Drugs,

Deals,

Delivered!

with

Sheila Hollands

Ernie Hollands Hebron Ministries, Inc.,
P.O. Box 1505
London, Ontario, Canada N6A 5M2

© ERNIE HOLLANDS-HEBRON MINISTRIES INC.

Published by
Ernie Hollands-Hebron Ministries Inc.,
P.O. Box 1505, London, Ontario, Canada N6A 5M2

The Master's Foundation
1290 Eglinton Ave. E., Suite 5, Mississauga, ON, Canada, L4W 1K8

ISBN - 1-895918-38-3

Printed in Canada

This book is dedicated
To my late husband,
Ernie Hollands, 1930 – 1996,
On the tenth annniversary of his "Homegoing,"
Who found true freedom
Through Jesus Christ,
After serving 25 years in prisons
Across Canada and the United States of America,
and to
All inmates worldwide
Who will find
This same freedom
As they believe
In The Lord Jesus Christ.

Sheila Hollands

iii

IN APPRECIATION

*To the six men who have shared their life
stories in this book.
The purpose of these difficult stories
is that others might be
saved, healed and restored.*

*To all who came alongside to make this
book possible.*

*To all who have given to make the
publication of this a reality.*

CONTENTS

PERSONAL PROLOGUE

It was in January 2005 that God spoke to me
about this book.
I waited on His direction.
Through His guidance of circumstances,
God has brought to us
each person who shares their life stories in this book.

The "Master Plan" for this book.
unfolds in each story
as some share their aboriginal ancestory.

I believe this book will bring hope and freedom to all
Canadians!
Three percent of our population is First Nations,
Yet the First Nations percentage in our prisons is 20%!
If God could change the lives recorded here,
these percentages can be changed!
Whatever your heritage,
Red or Yellow, Black or White
You are *Precious* in His Sight.

I am so pleased Jesus Christ didn't save us with His
Skin but with His Blood!
We all have red blood flowing through our bodies.

Bill and Joanne, 1995

Chapter One

COCAINE,

CANINE,

CHALLENGE!

The Life
of
Bill Smith

Cocaine, Canine, Challenge!

The year is 1996, the month is January, and it is Friday the 26th. Business is booming. All of a sudden, the New Westminster Drug Task Force breaks down the door of my house. Now there are about ten policemen, some dressed like Ninjas, their bodies completely covered except for their hands. As they surprised us, they shouted, "Police!" This upset my dog, Joanne, or as I affectionately called her, Jo. She started to bite the officer's hand. Everything was happening so fast, but in another way, it felt like it was going in slow motion. The other policemen are watching the dog. I called the dog away. She was coming to me when I heard 'pop' and a moment later she dropped, and fell on her side. The next thing I saw was blood coming from under her body. The other cops were busy securing the place, and arresting people. I had my .380 automatic in the side of my pants. I pulled it out and aimed it at the cop. Then I heard "that voice again". I put the gun back in my pocket. With so much going on in the room, no one saw my actions, or I would have been blown away. When they arrested me, I flopped on the bed with my hands up. While they were searching me, I managed to drop my arm to my side, get the gun from my pocket and stuff it under the pillow. Jo, my Doberman, dragged herself into the bedroom. Her one eye was all black, probably from an internal injury. I begged the police to shoot her and put her out of her pain, but they ignored me. How had I allowed life to come to this?

It certainly wasn't my family's fault. My father was a good man, who provided for his family. He was born in Hamilton, Ontario, Canada in 1937. His father had come from Poland, and named himself William Douglas Smith. When I was born on November 12, 1960 in the city of Hamilton, Ontario, I was given the same name. My dad didn't do drugs, and I never saw him drunk. His only bad habit was that he smoked cigarettes. He worked for Wonder Bread

Bakeries for thirty five years from 1949-1984 in Hamilton, and later in London, Ontario.

My mother was a wonderful Scottish woman. She was a housekeeper, and was at home raising her children. She would do anything for us. Mother had five children, four boys and one girl. The girl was the youngest. I was in the middle, the third child from my mother, but the first born from my father. My mother had two boys who were adopted out before she met my father. I never met James or Joseph. My mother taught us by example, and she did not do drugs, or drink, or smoke. She taught us good values. She would tell me, "Billy, if you don't have anything good to say about somebody, then do not say anything at all." Yes, I came from a good family.

In 1963, when I was just two and half years old, my mother and father decided that I should go to Sunday School. They sent us to the Gospel Hall on Kensington Avenue in Hamilton. That church is still there to this day. There was a Sunday School teacher, Miss Davison and she would pick us up every Sunday. My mother would dress her children up really nicely in dress pants, shirts, ties, and jackets. Our shoes were polished and our hair combed. Mom and dad never went to church, only to the Sunday School Picnic, once a year. I heard all the good stories from the Bible like David and Goliath, Samson and Delilah, Moses and the Ten Commandments, King Saul, and King David. I heard about Jesus, and that he was the Son of God. I believed around the age of six or seven that Jesus died for the sins of the world and was raised from the dead. I went to Sunday School until I was over eleven years of age.

When I was ten years old, I became interested in sports. I really enjoyed hockey. I was pretty good at it. Whenever we would pick teams, I was usually in the top three chosen for the team. I remember coming home from Sunday School all dressed in my Sunday best clothes. I would run into the house, change my clothes, grab my hockey stick, and run back outside to play with my friends. When we came home from Sunday School, Miss Davison had to drive right through the parking lot where my friends would be playing hockey. Then one day, when I was getting out of the car with my brother, David, and sister, Donna, my friends were mocking me. They were bugging me about being a sissy and going to Sunday School. It really bothered me. They had done this before, but this Sunday it was really bad. I ran into the house to change my clothes, and said to my mother and father, "I don't want to go to Sunday School anymore." They responded, "But you really should go to Sunday School." I reasoned, "I'm a really good hockey player, and it's my heart's desire to play hockey."

Mom and dad said, "It's okay to play hockey, but you need Sunday School too."

I told them, "My friends don't go, and they bug me, and I don't want to go anymore."

They said, "Your friends should go, but they don't go because they aren't interested."

There was something in me, and I looked at them, and I said, "But you don't go!"

What I said must have cut my mom and dad so deeply. It must have hurt them, because that day, they actually released me from going to Sunday School. For those nine years, from two to eleven years of age, I had been a decent kid. I was a "Straight A" student in school. I had so much going for me because of the Word of God in my life.

I made up my mind that I wanted my friends and hockey, and started to hang with the crowd. Miss Davison did try to encourage me back every Sunday, but I ignored her. I was now twelve years old. I was free to do my own thing. That same year, I took my first smoke and drank my first beer. Another thing happened that I will mention later in this story. I also did my first armed robbery when I was twelve. It happened at a variety store. I held them up with a knife, and was arrested shortly thereafter. I was sent to Arrow Observation Home. This was a detention centre for children while they waited to go to court. My father was ashamed of his son and would tell me I was trashing the family name. My father only had a grade one education. He was born just before World War II. In the 1930's earning a living and surviving was more important than education. He and his brother had a paper route of over one thousand people and they contributed their pay to the finances of the home. Mother had no education. Neither mom nor dad could read, and all they could write was their names. They couldn't read God's Word, so how could they help me? Maybe that was why they didn't want to go to church. Now my mother and father had to go to court. The court investigated them to see if they were unfit parents. They couldn't find anything wrong with them, and the other children listened and obeyed. The Children's Aid checked out our home. Mom kept a spotless home, dishes were washed, and cutlery shiny. The only thing lacking in our home was my parents had no education.

They couldn't understand why I was doing these things, like robbing with a knife. I was sent to Oakville Assessment Centre to see if I had other issues. It was decided for the best interest of society that I should go to a training school. I was sent to Brookside Training School in Cobourg, Ontario. I didn't like the place. I went to school for a bit, but I wasn't into it anymore. My friends taught me that school was not 'cool,' and I allowed my friends to influence my life. I was in this training school for about a year, and earned my way up to getting a pass to go home to visit my family. I enjoyed my week at home, and returned to Brookside.

Shortly after that, my graduation from training school happened. I had to take this paper to each department and get them to sign it. Everyone was shaking my hand and congratulating me. I never graduated from anything, so this made me feel good. It made me feel like somebody!

I returned home, and within a month I was hanging with the wrong crowd again, and I was making bad choices. I stole a truck, and got on a dead end street, and had no choice but to stop. The police arrested me, and I was sent back to the training school. I worked my way to graduation again. This time, they decided to send me to a group home. First I went to a receiving home. They wanted me to be adopted into a different family. My parents were against that, and wanted me to come home. Since I had been in training school, I was now a ward of the courts, and I was their responsibility until I was eighteen years old.

I was fourteen, so they sent me to this home that was run by two single men. They never tried anything with me. The one man liked to smoked pot – marijuana – so we got into smoking a lot more. I did learn some responsibilities at this place, like looking after my own room and laundry. Mother had always taken care of those things at home. I decided to return home.

Again, I started hanging around and was caught in a stolen vehicle, but this time I was put in jail. I was now sixteen years old. I was put in with a lot of men. I talked to my dad by telephone. He went and got the money from the bank, and posted the bail for me about 2:00 pm. I didn't get released until 8:00 pm. As soon as I walked out the front door, I saw my dad. There were two other men. I didn't recognize them at first. They were from Brookside. They took me in the van back to the training school. Dad bailed me out, and they took me. I was mad, and I told the staff at Brookside that I wouldn't go to school, so they offered me a job as the postman. I would ride this bike around to the houses on Brookside's property to deliver the mail. There were four houses for guys, and two for girls. Then one day, we were playing baseball, and I was hanging with the wrong crowd. We decided we would take off. All three of us were caught, and put in cells. The superintendent came and spoke to me. He asked me, "Are you ever going to change your ways?" I remembered my mother would often ask this question. Now, Joe, who really cared, was asking me this same question.

I couldn't live at home anymore. They had rules and I was breaking them. I went to a group home called "Real Life Incorporated" in London, Ontario. (My family now lived in London, Ontario, since Wonder Bread Bakeries had relocated, and had moved our family.) The staff at this new place was Christian-based. My heart had been hardened over the years. Bob, and his wife, Doris, lived in the home like house parents. One day, they took me to a church building. There was another man there, a minister. The three of them and I sat and talked. They asked questions about different things that had happened to me. They weren't judgmental. I felt at ease. We had been talking a long time when they asked me if I had ever been sexually assaulted. I looked at them for awhile and then felt I could talk about it. I had never told anyone about this, not even my parents. I told them that it had happened when I was twelve years old. He was a neighbour. He offered my friends and me a drink. Then he gave us so many drinks that we passed out drunk. I remember waking up with no clothes on. It was weird. It was terrible. It had really affected me, and I believe it led to my becoming so rebellious. They prayed against these things, and asked me to pray for forgiveness, and to forgive this man who had done this to me. They also prayed for healing for my body. These things really impressed me. At the end of the day after lots of prayer, we went back to the group home. Bob and Doris were always encouraging the six of us who lived there, in God's Ways. There was a lot of the Lord's light in this home. I got work at a bakery while at this group home. One night while I was sweeping up crumbs, as I bent over to do this, my cigarettes and matches fell out of my uniform pocket and landed in the dustpan. I stopped and was putting down the broom to pick up my cigarettes, when I heard that voice, "if you throw out your cigarettes you will never smoke again." I listened, and never smoked cigarettes again.

Some time later, I decided to buy a bag of marijuana, and smoked a few joints. Just like that, I decided that I didn't want to live there anymore. Being confronted by them because of my actions, I left and got the train to Toronto. I got off at Burlington, and headed to Hamilton, but then I was on the run, since I was still a ward the province. I drank, and did drugs, and after a while it got to be boring. I was losing my friends. Every time we committed a crime, we would lose a few more guys to the police. The gang was down from twenty to four. I decided to turn myself in. I took the train to Cobourg, and called the training school. They came and got me from the train station, and locked me up. It didn't bother me. I got some rest, and got away from the drugs and booze. About three weeks later, Bill, from Real Life Incorporated in Hamilton came to Brookside, and offered to take me back to London, but I refused. He could not understand. I chose lock-up over freedom. I believe I was becoming institutionalized at this young age. We escaped from Brookside, and broke into the nearby variety store. What could they do to us? All we got was another crime against our name. At Brookside, we would be taken to different churches in town every Sunday. I think the people at this place were Christians, and tried to do the best for us, but all these churches were so different. It was confusing. I graduated, but now I was seventeen.

I got a parole officer, and I was to see him every two weeks. He was a pretty mean guy. I probably put some of that nastiness in him because of my rebellious actions. I was supposed to have a meeting with him, but I didn't go. He came into the pool hall where I was playing, and he told me I was supposed to be at his office. I told him I would go when the game was over. He grabbed the balls and pushed them in the pockets. He told me the game was over, and so I had to go with him. Another time, I hadn't seen him for three months. I decided to show up at his office. He pointed to the papers on his desk, and he told me that all that was needed was his signature to send me back to Brookside. He told me he was going to sign them, but first he wanted to know why I hadn't come in to see him for three months. He told me if I lied to him, he would sign them and I would be on the way back to Brookside for another year, until I was eighteen. If I told him the truth, he would rip up those papers and give me another chance. I decided to tell the truth. I told him that I was too darn lazy to come. I just didn't want to come. I was too busy doing my thing. He believed I was telling the truth, and he tore up my papers. This really impressed me. If I told the truth, it would set me free.

It wasn't long before I was in trouble again, and served six months provincial time in Burtch Correctional Centre. Then I did another twelve months in Maplehurst Institution in Milton, Ontario. Following another break and enter, I was in possession of stolen property, and received another twenty-three months. I was back again on Unit 4, the working unit, as I worked in the kitchen.

I had served about sixteen months of the twenty-three month sentence. It was a Friday, and I received a letter from my dad. It told me that my grandmother was dying and in the hospital and they didn't think she would make it until Friday. Now this was my only grandparent. This was my dad's mother. My mother's mother died before I was born. Actually her husband killed her. Grandfather Jones liked to drink, and they were arguing, and he gave her a push. She fell down the stairs and didn't survive. She was pregnant with her sixteenth child. This grandmother, dad's mother, had nine children with her first husband and after his death, married a Mr. Smith, and had seven children with him. After his death, she married another Mr. Smith. My dad was a child from the second husband. When we had a funeral in the family, it was large. I liked Grandmother Smith, because she always loved me. I showed this letter to a guard, and told him that my grandmother might die today, and I would like to go to see her, and asked if I could get a pass. They said that they would think about it. The next day, Saturday, I read in the obituary page of the newspaper about my grandmother's death, and my name was in the list of the grandchildren. I took it and showed the guard and asked if I could go to the funeral. It was only twenty-five miles from the prison. They were thinking of letting me go, but had to verify it with my parents. They telephoned my parents in London, Ontario, but they had already left for Hamilton. They called four or five times on Saturday and again on Sunday, but got no reply. I think if my father had called the prison they would have let me go. The funeral was Monday, and the lieutenant made one more phone call and still there was no answer. I couldn't take it anymore, and flipped out. I was a big twenty years old, 6' 3 and 240 lbs. I started to fight with this guard. He took off to get back to the secure office, where the other guards were sitting. He started screaming and running up the stairs, and I tackled him. I grabbed his tie, but it was one of those clip-on ties, and I fell down. He made it into the office. I started beating on the windows. The guys on the unit started chanting "Go, Smith, Go!" I saw they were on the telephone, and knew they were calling the riot squad. I barricaded the door by pushing sofas and chairs against the door. There were about 104 guys in the unit. They started to pass me the chairs to put at the door. I went back and beat on the window again. I had the guards terrified. Eventually, the Assistant Superintendent came and said he would try to contact my father if I would calm down. He said that he wanted to see me over in Unit 3. I believed him! I took everything away from the door. I walked down the corridor. I was all on my own now. I passed the segregation unit. Then just as I passed the gym doors, the segregation door flew open, and the riot squad grabbed me, and threw me in the hole for three days. When they came to let me out, they said the same thing that had been said on the TV Show "Cool Hand Luke" "Your grandmother is dead and buried now, and so we are letting you out, you better behave yourself." They threatened to send me to Millbrook. I didn't care where I did time.

I was only out five months, and I was back again

at Maplehurst in Unit 4. One of the guards remembered me from the previous time. This time I was more subdued. I was getting sick and tired of doing time. He suggested that I ask for a pass. He told me that I seemed like a nice guy, and that I minded my own business. He told me that he would recommend me for a pass. I seemed to be getting mixed messages from people, but put in for a three day pass. They gave it to me. I had quite a bit of money in my prison account, and so I took out $500. I used it on drugs and alcohol. I was supposed to be back at the prison in another hour. I was wasted. I couldn't go back. Now I was on the run. I decided to go out West. We headed out in a stolen car. We arrived in Sault Ste. Marie in Northern Ontario using stolen credit cards. We went to the bar and got drunk. My buddy got in a fight with four guys. I stuck up for him. We left town and he drove the car into a six foot snow bank. The car disappeared. He was shouting, "Get out and run." I didn't know where we were going, but we ran. Eventually we ended up at a mechanic's garage. There was a tow truck in one of the work bays. I took the tow truck, and we were driving it down the road, and the cops were after us. We must have tripped some alarm. They caught us, and I was held in Sault Ste. Marie jail for four months. I remember that night well. I was soaked as I had been running through the snow banks. When they locked me up, I stripped down to my underwear, and rung out my wet clothes and hung them on the bars to dry. I then lay down on the bunk, as if I was home. I remember the policeman commenting to his partner, "This guy needs help." I pleaded guilty to being in possession of firearms, since there were guns in the car that we had stolen. I got another consecutive twenty-three months, and was shipped to London, Ontario. Here I pleaded guilty to the stolen car, and got another year added to my sentence. Next, I was shipped to Hamilton for being unlawfully at large and received six consecutive months.

Finally, they shipped me to the federal system in

Kingston where I spent some time in Collin's Bay Prison. Here they evaluated you as to your education. They asked me what grade I had graduated from in school, and I said, "Grade 12." I hadn't completed Grade 12, but didn't intend to go to school. They gave me tests. The guy beside me was an educated man. He would tell me the answers. I did fairly well at mathematics, so I could handle that. Then they gave me a personal evaluation to discover why I had done my crimes. My crimes were mostly theft. I was not a major danger to society. I was more a menace. They asked me why I had done these crimes. My friend had told me what to say, so I said that it was because I was homeless and needed food. This was the best possible answer to tell them. If I had mentioned alcohol and drugs, they would make me do programs.

Since I had waited so long to go to court, I was already passed my day parole time, so I was shipped to the camp outside Collin's Bay called Frontenac. Here I met a friend from Hamilton. He told me about a prison in Gravenhurst called Beavercreek. There were only 15 men there and they needed another twenty-five more to go there. I wasn't sure I wanted to transfer, but when he said there was a swimming pool there, I decided to go. It was quite nice. We went jogging and swimming each day. The black flies were bad! It was easier to get parole from here. I went to Peterborough, Ontario for my National Parole Board Hearing. I stuck to my story of hungry, homelessness, and got to eat. They bought into this. They asked me if I thought I could change. I remembered my mom, then Joe, the Superintendent at Brookside, and now the Parole Board asking me this question. Would I ever change? Could I ever change?

I ended up at St. Leonard's House. I had a girlfriend who was waiting for me while I was in jail. When I got out, I wanted to date her. Her dad was an AA (Alcoholics Anonymous) man. He started to ask me some questions. He asked me if I had ever considered AA. Then he gave me this paper with questions, as to how alcohol had affected my life and work. I thought the questions were very biased and that mostly people would have to answer "Yes" to most of those questions. I did go to one AA meeting just to keep on his good side since I was dating his daughter. I listened with interest at how they seemed to care for each other. I wasn't interested. Since I did not seek help, he told his daughter she could not date me, and so we drifted apart.

I met another girl. I now had a job. My only restriction at St. Leonard's House in Hamilton, were to obey the rules of the home. I had no drinking restriction. I would get drunk every Friday, but because I would go up to bed, and caused no problems, they didn't say much. A friend of mine was on staff, and we took a lot of liberties with the ladies from the bar. Then a new person was hired who had done time in the federal system, and slowly things began to change. I had sold and was using acid while at St. Leonard's. My connection was giving me 1000 hits of acid at a time – I would pay later. He connected me to some heavies. At one time, I owed him about 10,000 hits. I decided I wasn't going to pay him. It was going to get pretty ugly, so I went U.A.L. –unlawfully at large.

Five months, later I was at a gas station and there was an OPP (Ontario Provincial Police) officer there. I was in a truck. It was mine, but it had the wrong plates on it. I could see he was checking on my plates. Then he was following me. He put on his lights, and we were into a high speed chase from Clappison's Corners just outside of Hamilton to near Brantford, Ontario. I was going over 160 kilometres in my Ford truck. Soon, there were six police cruisers involved in the chase. There was no place to go so I bailed out of the truck in the country. The police decided to bring in the dogs and search the area where I had bailed out. I remember it was December 16. It was very cold. There was water there, and I could get in the water and lose the dogs. Did I want to go back to the joint, or get in the water? I didn't want to go back to prison, so I slowly walked into the water until it was up to my waist. Then when the police got closer with the dogs, I knelt down in the water, and slowly submerged myself. It was freezing. They passed by and I slowly came up for air. I had just my head out of the water, but then another policeman and dog came by, and this dog caught my scent and came into the water and grabbed me by the arm and pulled me out. I was taken to the Burlington OPP station and I gave them a phony name. They let me go, with a promise to appear in a week in Dundas, Ontario for fingerprinting and pictures. I figured these guys were dumb and I had outsmarted them.

Another couple of months passed, and this time Hamilton police got me. They knew me. I went to court for being unlawfully at large, and the break and entry. Then a cop from Burlington who was at court that day recognized me, so they tacked on charges for the high speed chase. I ended up in Millhaven back in the federal system, in Kingston, Ontario. I was processed through Collin's Bay Prison to Frontenac Farm which is minimum security. Here, I enjoyed playing ice hockey and ball hockey every night. I remember one night when we were having a game with Bath Institution (Millhaven's Minimum Farm Camp) and the score was twenty to sixteen. We won. In that game, I scored seventeen goals. The name "The Great One" was given to me. I was proud of this title. I knew I was a pretty good hockey player, but now I was recognized. Frontenac also had milking cows, beef cows, and chickens. I exchanged jobs so I could do general labour, so I didn't really have to work. Eighteen months later, I returned to Hamilton.

It was now 1986 and I decided I wasn't going back to prison. I met this lady, Dee, and we moved in together. She was on a disability pension as a result of open heart surgery. I got a job. We both did a fair amount of drinking. Her mother died, and she took it very badly. When we went to the funeral, she wanted me to hold her. I didn't know how to feel. I had no feelings left after my years of incarceration. Her mother had liked me, and made me promise to care for Dee.

I was working at this job delivering eggs, cheese, and meats to the hospital. I had to deliver goods to St. Leonard's House. They were amazed that I was doing so well. I was called the "Marathon Man" at D.A. Warrings – because I did deliveries so quickly. I got some raises, and was enjoying my job. No one knew my past history of prisons or training school. We always had enough money. I was still drinking, and trying to keep out of trouble at the bars. One night, I was at Copper Johns with Dee, and this other man who worked at the same company as I did, was there. He picked an argument with me, and challenged me from across the bar. I went to the door and suggested we take it outside. He backed down. After a couple more drinks, he decided that he would take me on. We moved outside. I didn't expect to win, since he was bigger than me, but I got in a good shot, which knocked him out. When he went down, he really went down hard. When he got up his speech was slurred. I left. I went to the next bar. My friends followed me, and told me the cops were looking for me, since the man had gone to the hospital in an ambulance. I took off out of the bar. The next day was my day off, and the cops came to my job to find me. I had been out of trouble for a couple of years, and I was feeling very badly. I told my employer that I was leaving. He said that he as an employer would help me work it out, but I was paranoid about spending more years back in jail. I told Dee it was time to move. We used my truck and a U-Haul and packed up our belongings. My dad was sad to see me move. He had come to respect me as a productive member of society. He helped load up the truck. He had smoked all his life. He seemed short of breath. I told him to rest but he kept working until everything was done. When I said goodbye to dad, that would be the last time I would see him alive. Some time later, he died of a heart attack.

Dee had lived out West before, and so we headed out West in 1989. We stopped in Medicine Hat, Alberta as Dee's sister and husband lived there. That day, we found an apartment, and moved in the next day. The following day I got a job working the pipeline. I worked at that job until it came to an end. I worked a number of jobs over the next couple of years. I have been stopped by police for traffic violations, but there was no warrant out for me. I now had a good union job and was ready to work there until I retired. We had a nice home. We both had cars. I had a truck, three motorcycles, a boat and trailer. Everything was going well but still I felt empty.

Some people came to my door and so I studied with them in my home for a couple of months. At first I liked what they had to say. Dee would go and walk the dog, or do something in the house, while I would talk with them. Then one day, this book we were studying said that Jesus and Adam were equal. Something inside me said, "No way!" What little knowledge I had from Sunday School came back to help me. I saw through their lies. I told them not to come to my house anymore. I asked Dee if she ever thought about God. She said that she already had found God. She was Anglican. We had been living together for five years, and so I confronted her with that fact, and also mentioned our lack of faith. From that point on Dee and I seemed to slowly drift apart. I was searching to fill this void in my life.

Then the Americans came and bought the company I worked for and dismissed us. They hired non-unionized workers. I got depressed because of a lack of work, and started eating six meals or more a day. My weight soared to 320 lbs. My unemployment benefits were coming to an end, so we left Medicine Hat. We left our home, moved to Edmonton, and lived in a hotel. The relationship fell apart, and we parted. We sold the house and divided our possessions. We had raised a Doberman, Joanne, since she was a puppy, and I kept her. Finally, Dee moved into a nice home with Cam, an electrician. They took care of Joanne on one occasion when I had to be out of town with my new job. Dee decided that she was going to keep the dog. I went to the police and ask them to get the dog back for me. The police telephoned her. I stood and watched the policeman's face change from compassion for me to a very stern expression. I could only imagine what she was telling him. She probably told him about the eleven years in prisons and training schools, the drinking and the assault. He then told her that possession was 9/10 of the law, and to keep the dog. I screamed at the policeman. Another officer came and told me to leave or I would get arrested.

I even got a lawyer's advice. He told me it would be very expensive. He also gave me the idea that if I could find out where she lived, I could get the dog when she was outside some day. I went in search of the house, and found it. I telephoned and spoke to Dee, and Cam came on the other line and told me he wasn't giving back the dog. I told him that if they didn't return Joanne, I would come and knock in the doors, and take him on, and then take my dog. They said that I didn't know where they lived. I gave them the address. The line went dead. Dee must have given him my track record because he called back, and Joanne was returned to me. This was the last time I heard from Dee.

Later, I met another lady named Sandi from Edmonton. We lived a number of places over the next couple of years, Prince Rupert, New Westminster, and Calgary. My brother, sister and family had moved to Calgary. Sandi wanted to visit her mother in Edmonton, so we drove up from Calgary. I dropped her off at her mother's place, and went to hang out with my friends. It was Friday afternoon, so we went to the liquor store. I went in and got what I needed. My friend had a lot of empties to return and was pleased I had a car to get them there. I was waiting in the car when this man came to my car and asked for a $1. I told him I didn't have one, since I had no change. He called me names. I got out of my car, and asked him if he wanted a piece of me. He saw my size and decided he wouldn't fight. I got back in the car. He changed his mind, and so I got back out of the car, and it wasn't long before I had him down. It was March, and the snow was melting, and there was about four inches of water in the gutter. I had him face down in the water. I was holding him down. Then I heard two others yelling for me to let him go. Next thing they wanted to fight, and so I took them on. Then there was a third and fourth guy challenging me. There were just too many people. I got to the car, and popped the trunk and got out this steel bar which was my jack handle. I started to whack these guys. There was this woman with crutches and she was yelling, "Get his plate number". All of a sudden this guy came around the corner. He was a huge guy. Everyone cheered saying that I was going to get it now. He walked right up to me. The adrenalin was flowing because of all the guys, and so I said to him, "Do you want a piece of this pipe?" He said that he did. I whacked him with all my strength in the head. The blood started squirting out, and his eyes rolled back, and he fell to the ground very hard. The lady with the crutches gave them to the guys and told them to get me. I ran for my car. Now I was trying to make it out of the parking lot without running into anyone. They kept blocking the exits. Finally I made it through, but someone hit the window of my Malibu with the crutches, and it shattered all over my friend in the passenger's seat, and my dog in the back seat. I went to my buddy's house. I was pretty shaken up. I think he was sorry for the long time he took in the store, and for staying in there while the fight was on, so he decided to vacuum up the broken glass. The next day I replaced the window in the car since it was winter. Then I picked up Sandi and drove back to Calgary.

We lived in a duplex. I rented a room to a guy, and he was there when we got home. I told him a little about what had happened in Edmonton. About 8:30 pm I saw five police cruisers closing in. I told Sandi and Jeff not to rat (give any information) me out. I disappeared behind the adjoining laundry. They questioned them about this being Bill Smith's place, and the car in the driveway that was registered to Bill Smith. They made up some story that they had just moved in, and the car was to be picked up by the previous owner. The cops checked the car. The window was fine, and so they left. I called the liquor store in Edmonton and found out the man was in a coma. I took Sandi to her mother's in Edmonton the next day. I was very nervous in case the police spotted me. I came back to Calgary. The next day I sold everything in a garage sale for $3200. I packed my car and left for Ontario.

I was drinking heavily to forget everything, because I knew I could get life if this man died. Three weeks later, Sandi telephoned to tell me that the man was out of the coma. The police had asked him who was responsible for his injury. He was solid, and told them that he would look after this himself. I came back to Edmonton and picked up Sandi, and we decided to go through to British Columbia, to Sapperton. My girlfriend, Sandi, was a First Nations native. Dee had not been able to have children. Now Sandi was pregnant. I was finally going to be a father. She started to hang around some of her friends. I think they told her that she shouldn't have my baby. Without telling me, she got an abortion. Things just fell apart. I felt so betrayed.

All this time, I was working for John, doing racking. It's construction, so there was work, and then there was none. It was during one of these no work periods that I met Luke from our old apartment building. He was into drugs. I decided to invest $500 in cocaine. I started to sell it out of my car, and in twelve hours, I made $1000 clear. I went back and did it for a few nights. I met this friend, and he said that if I gave him some money, I could sell from his house. This was a lot better than selling from a car. I moved to another house, and things expanded, until I was selling from four or five houses. I wasn't using drugs myself.

Welfare Wednesday was coming up, and I knew I needed to stay awake over the next three days to do my deals, and so I smoked a rock. I stayed awake. I kept using and dealing drugs. I was making money, and buying stupid things, like Rambo knives, percussion grenades, and guns.

19

John called me to come back to work. I told him that I was busy with another job, and would contact him in a month. I couldn't see myself going back to work when I could make big money with drugs.

Then one day Johnny came to my house. He free based cocaine. He smoked away his Camero, Harley Davidson, and everything he owned. I got all that money. I smoked it and shared it with the different ladies. The ladies were always there to get free cocaine for favours. Johnny owed me money. I hadn't seen him for a couple of months. Then he came to my house with this huge guy, I will call him C. C gave me a roll of money and said he was straightening up for Johnny. My doorman told me that he was a "patch", a biker. I knew this meant trouble. The next day he came back. He hung around and saw the amount of traffic. He suggested that he had some product and we could work a deal. Next time, he brought me a gift, an ounce of cocaine, which was $1100 in value. I gave him gifts of some stolen stuff, cameras, and belt buckles of approximately the same value. I knew bikers played hard, and I could die if I got involved. Then he came back with a pound of cocaine. I didn't know how I could say no, so I created this plan. I suggested that a couple of the ladies wanted to meet him. I figured that when he came out of the bedroom after two hours with these two women, after drinking some Jack Daniels, that I would take my shot at saying no, and at least I would live. He came out and thanked me and wanted an answer. I told him that at this time I would have to say no. He wasn't too pleased but accepted my answer. I thought, "I am still alive. I better sell, sell, sell, and get out of here." By now I was a full blown free base coconut. My three day runs were now into five, six or seven day runs. I would bug right out. I would be walking into a wall, losing track of money, losing track of drugs. The ladies and doormen were all opportunists wanting to take money and dope. I decided to try heroin. The first day I tried it, I nearly overdosed. I snorted a whack of it. I wasn't into shooting any needles into my arms. I didn't get off. I didn't realize it took a little bit to kick in, so I smoked some and both kicked in. I couldn't stand up. I didn't like this at all. I liked to be in control. This was dangerous business. It still amazes me that all the times when I was out cold, nobody snuffed out my life. I would be knocked out for twenty-six hours. I would have a couple of guys selling for me. The guys would want to come into my room to get another quarter, half, or ounce, but my Doberman would just growl. She protected me. People were terrified of my dog, as she would bite on command. Anyway, biker buddy was gone, but I figured I could get a bullet in the back of my head anytime. The "real" Bill, inside, was saying, "I got to get out of here". I went down to 195 lbs. I am 6' 3" – and I should be 240 lbs. I would smoke an ounce of cocaine a day. I would do a forty dollar blast in one pipe, and forty dollar in another pipe. By attaching the two pipes together with a hose that had holes in it, I would do this eighty dollar hoot. The smoke would fill the whole room. I remember my dog sitting by my side watching the smoke. Through her eyes, I saw my dog questioning me, "Are we ever going to get out of here, are you ever going to change?" I heard those words again from my mother and Joe from Brookside. We, Jo and I, used to have a great life. We'd go to the parks. Now, I didn't even take her out. Other people were doing that for me. I loved her, but I was neglecting her. I was living in this lovely large home, but would just live in one room with my drugs. I was never without dope. I would go to my dealer everyday and buy a pound of dope. I would call him on his pager, and dial in my number, #14, and then I would enter 10,000. This meant I was bringing $10,000 in cash. We would always meet me in the lobby, and get on the elevator. I would hand him the bag with the money, and he would give me the bag with the dope. He was solid. We didn't check what was in the bag. We trusted each other. The elevator would stop at the second floor, and he would get off. I would return to the ground floor and leave. It took less than three minutes.

I knew it was only a matter of time. I couldn't get out of this alive. I was a slave to these drugs. In desperation, I cried out to Jesus, "Lord Jesus, get me out of here! Help me! I am stuck in this room." Jesus did help me. A short time later, He sent the police to get me out of there.

The Drug Task Force from New Westminster arrived and the drug bust went down, and my dog was shot by the police. I pulled out my gun and aimed it at that cop, but heard that voice, "If you pull the trigger you will spend eternity separated from Me." I put the gun back in my pocket. I believe God prevented the cops from seeing that gun, or I would have been blown away. I asked them to put Joanne out of her pain, but they refused. I had managed to throw the drugs out the window as they broke through the door. The drugs disappeared in the fallen snow. They showed me the warrant. It had David Smith on it. They were a little concerned since I was Billy Smith. Then they found identification for both David and Billy Smith in the house. They ransacked the house, and found money everywhere: $3,100 in the garlic spice container, $1700 in the Cornflake box, and $700 in a dirty sock in the closet. The final tally was $53,000. They also found my box with twenty-four Rambo knives at $400 each, guns, a bullet proof vest, and many more items. They strip searched all nine of us, the girls in the bathroom and the men in the bedroom. Finally, as they were taking us out to the cruiser, they asked for permission to shoot the dog, after she had suffered for forty minutes. I gave permission. I saw them put her in a garbage bag. I didn't know how much all this would affect me. As we left, they asked if the Honda was mine. I denied it, and they didn't check it. There were assault rifles in it. They arrested four of us that Friday night.

Monday I made bail, and ran home. The house had been ransacked by the police, and then the drug users had cleaned the place out. I put my hand in my dog's blood and sobbed. In my mind's eye, I replayed the movie of what had happened that night. This went on for three days. The drug users coming by comforted me.

I started selling again, as I knew I needed money to leave town. I had a plan. I went to the first appearance in court, and then the second appearance. This had given me time to accumulate $74,000. I flew to Edmonton. I tried to sell dope, but I couldn't. I had to have drugs, and so my finances kept dropping. I was drinking and having a pity party. I was down to $15,000.

One day I became suicidal! I didn't see how I could take a job for twenty dollars an hour when I could make $6000 a day. I flew to Vancouver and called the New Westminster Police Station, and asked for the Drug Task Force. I got the answering machine. I left a message for the Constable. I said, "I am the owner of the dog that you shot three months ago. I am bitter and angry, and I am packing, and I can snuff out your life, so watch out!" I figured that they would come after me. I was suicidal. I felt that if I committed suicide, I would never see God, but if they took my life, then I might have a chance. Nothing happened the first night. The next day as I walked down the street, a druggie told me that the cops were looking for me. They had my photo in their cruisers. All of a sudden, I didn't want to die. I went over to Sapperton and laid low. My friend was solid. He would go out and get drugs. He got questioned, but said nothing. The police were offering a $2000 reward to anyone who would turn me in. Many would have sold me out, but my friend didn't. I was down to $4000, so I jumped on a plane back to Edmonton.

In thirty days, I was broke. I went to Welfare and told them I had lost my identification. I didn't tell them that I had lost it to the police. They gave me $400, and I got low income housing for $155. I was just trying to survive. After the first month, they asked me to be caretaker, so my housing cost only $100. I was lying low, and drinking. The devil was playing mind games with me. He told me I was just a loser,

Vance Mcphail, Bill Smith and Ken Hunchak

and that I had no friends. My mom and dad were dead. He suggested that I should just end things, and kill myself.

Down the street was this Mustard Seed Church. I started to hang out there because you could get free food. Friday nights were special because Vance & Ken would come in with their team. They would ask Bible questions, and if you got the answers, you got prizes, usually snack food. After about a month or two, Vance came to talk to me. I started to pour out my whole story to him. He listened. He was a good listener. Ken would come by, in between caring for the other one hundred and fifty in the room, and say "Billy, you need Jesus." I trusted Vance. I even told him I was on the run from the police. I told him about my years in jail. I told him I didn't want to live anymore.

Vance and Ken gave me work opportunities. Vance had a farm south of Edmonton, and he would get me to fix the fences. He was also a physiotherapist. He helped people even if they didn't have money to pay for the treatment. I would enjoy being at the farm. I would feel a peace and calm when I was there. When he paid me, and I was back at the housing, I'd be on drugs and booze. Vance and Ken saw me when I was drunk, and stoned, and also when I was happy, sad, and depressed. Both Vance and Ken attended this Calvary Southside Church. They would go on Sunday and ask the people in their church to pray for Billy, who was suicidal.

The devil was out to destroy me. He was playing those mind games. One night, I was down on my knees with two exacto knives in my hands, held up to my jugular vein in my throat. I was shaking. I had my doors locked. In desperation, I cried out "Jesus I know you are real, but I still feel compelled to take my life. Help me!" Immediately, there was a knock at the door. I thought I was hearing things, but I realized that someone was at the door. It was Joseph, this First Nations guy. He lived in my apartment building. He told me he didn't have a clue why he was knocking on my door, but wondered if I was okay. I told him that I was about to kill myself, but because he came just at the right moment, my life was spared.

I started to search for the Lord right after that happened. There are a lot of places one can go to hear the Good News and get fed, too. I would be in ten meetings a week. Then one Friday night, Vance and Ken asked me if I had found the Lord, since I had been looking for Him for some three to four months. They told me that God is everywhere, so they wondered why I hadn't found Him. I knew about God from Sunday School, and that He was everywhere. It was a real puzzle to me why I hadn't found Him. I went home and did a real inner search. I decided that there were three things keeping me from God. The next Friday, when they asked me the same question, I told them that I haven't found God because, one, I was too full of pride. They asked me what would make me humble. I thought, and declared probably if someone would truly beat me up. Then they asked me what was reason two. I told them that I needed to hear someone speak God's Word with power and authority. Finally, I would have to know someone who had a worse life than myself.

That week I was pressuring this woman who owed me twenty dollars. This man stood up for her. I swung at him and hit him in the jaw. Usually, I knocked people out. This did not fizz on this man. I dropped my hands to my sides wondering why he was still standing. He came onto me. I tried to bring my hands up, but I couldn't. It seemed that someone was holding them down. I heard that voice again, "You need to be humble to come to Me. You said that losing a fight would humble you. Watch this." This man punched and booted me. I was going to fall down, but couldn't move, and so he pounded me some more. I believe God send his angels to hold my arms down, and to hold me up. Finally, since I didn't fall down, he got tired and left. I was black and blue, bruised, with black eyes. When I arrived at the Mustard Seed on Friday night, they looked at me, and asked what had happened. I told them that someone half my size had beaten me up and that I was truly humbled.

Two nights later, I was talking to some drug users on the street, and they said that they were going over to this church on 101 Street. They told me that the pastor's wife made excellent Sloppy Joes after the meeting. I decided to go. It was this little place underneath the Bluenose Hotel.

Pastor Larry Nelson had a strong American accent, but had been born in Calgary, Alberta. He and his father had both served in the Marines. After we had gathered in the building, he would shut the doors. He spoke with authority. He told us there would be no walking around during the service. Only the Holy One, the Holy Spirit would be moving around. He played the guitar from his heart, and would even weep while he was singing. He would tell us that Our Papa loves us and sent His son, Jesus, to die for us. He spoke with authority about God from His Word. I could feel God's power in that place. I would cry, but try not to show it. At the end of service, he called for us to come and kneel down before the Lord, and ask Him to forgive our sins. I wouldn't kneel down. The next week I went again. I also enjoyed the Sloppy Joes. This happened for five weeks. I told Ken and Vance on Friday night about these meetings. They reminded me that I had been humbled, and now I had heard the Word of God with authority. They prayed that I would meet the person whose life was worse than mine. In the sixth week, I returned to Pastor Larry's church, and heard more about Jesus, his life, his death, and resurrection. The next week, when I saw Ken and Vance, I told them I met the person who had a life worse than mine. It was Jesus. They were so happy, and asked me if I was now a Christian. I said, "No". I told them there was a fourth thing. I wanted them to be there the next Sunday as I gave my life to Jesus. They came and sat with me, as Pastor Larry spoke with power and authority. I went forward and knelt before the Lord and asked Jesus in my Life. There were two of us who decided for Christ that day. It was August 18, 1996. I was thirty-five years old. I went there feeling so heavy, but after that prayer, I felt so light, I had such peace and deep joy. Even God's creation was brighter, the skies more blue, the grass greener. I felt so alive. There wasn't that need for drugs and alcohol. I was truly set free. The next week, we were baptized in water. They had a metal watering trough. The water was cold. When Pastor Larry submerged me –in the name of the Father, Son and Holy Spirit- the water overflowed the tank. He stated that God had placed an 'overflowing calling' on my life. I couldn't get enough of God's Word – I would read the Bible eight to nine hours a day. I spent lots of time at Pastor Larry's church. I helped to paint the place. This went on for about seven weeks.

Then again, I heard that voice. I now realized it was God's voice. He had been speaking to me all through the years. God's voice told me, "Go to British Columbia and turn yourself into police, for the false identification, the guns, the failure to appear in court, the death threats, and P.P.T. (Possession for the Purpose of Trafficking), and I will be with you". I told Ken and Vance about this. They felt it was the right thing to do. I knew I could be looking at five to ten years, but I had to trust God. Ken and Vance took me to the airport. They arranged for Allan with M2 – W2 (Man to Man – Woman to Woman) Prison Ministry to meet me when I got off the plane in Vancouver. I arrived on a Friday and Allan offered for me to come to his house for the weekend, and then turn myself in on Monday. I thought this was a kind offer, especially since he didn't know me. I thanked him but told him that I had come to turn myself in to the police. He asked if we could have a cup of coffee. I agreed. I was able to tell him about my old life and how God had changed me and given me a new life.

Then we went to the Surrey RCMP (Royal Canadian Mounted Police) Detachment so I could turn myself in. They asked for my identification, and I didn't have any. They refused to take me into custody. I didn't know what to do, so I left. Allan and I went to a payphone. I called the Detachment in New Westminster and asked for the Drug Task Force Department. I recognized the name of the constable who answered the phone as one who was at the drug bust at my apartment. I told him I wanted to turn myself in at Surrey but they wouldn't take me. I asked if he would make a telephone call to them. He was very pleased to do this. We walked back to the Surrey Detachment, and then they took me into custody.

I settled back into the routine in Surrey Pre-Trial. I started to do Gospel Echoes Bible Study Courses. Three guys approached me and one of them challenged me about my Bible Study courses, saying that I was a sissy to be doing them. I warned him, and he left. I spent most of my time with the patch holder/biker. The next day, the same three guys approached me. I wasn't going to let anyone distract me from God and His Word, this time. I stood my ground, and he was down in a minute. I was in segregation for fifteen days. The patch holder, who was in for a double life appeal, questioned me as to whether I was a Christian since I fought this guy. I told him their challenge, and how I let the old self rise up in me, since I was just a new Christian. Allan, from M2 – W2, arranged for a Jewish lawyer for me. We went for bail, but it was denied. The lawyer told me to wait thirty days, and he would get bail for me. Now the second of the three guys challenged me about my Bible Studies. We had it out. I spent another fifteen days in the hole. I didn't mind this as it gave me peace to read my Bible. I made bail on the second try.

I went to a Halfway House with very strict stipulations. I kept reading the Bible. They liked this as this was a 'religious' place. They wanted me to confess I was an alcoholic. I could not do this because Jesus had set me free and I was a new person. They felt I was making waves in their program. I could see this wasn't going to work out, so I asked to go back to jail. They made the call to the police. When they arrived they were surprised to see me. Most times the person had already taken off before the cruiser arrived. They allowed me to walk to the cruiser. Now back in Surrey Pre-Trial, I worked out on the weights with the patch holder, or played basketball in the gym. I was into my Bible, and over the Christmas period, was able to tell three guys how to let Jesus change their lives. Then the third one of those three guys challenged me. I didn't want to fight, but he kept at me. I knew the guards were watching and hoped they would make a move, but they didn't. I had no choice. It was over in a minute, and he was on the way to the hospital, and I was on my way to the hole for fifteen days. He got twenty stitches at the hospital, and spent three days in the hole. We apologized to each other while we were in the hole. While I was in the hole, I made up a song called, "Seven steps with Jesus, Seven steps with My Lord." I would sing this as I would pace the seven steps in the cell. One night I was singing, and as I approached the cell door, a guard walked by. He jumped! He said that he saw a ghost. I reassured him that it was only the Holy Ghost and me.

We went to court. They said if I plead guilty, they would give me seven years. My lawyer refused. He told me that we would beat these charges. It was remanded, and then I was offered a five year sentence. With each remand, the Crown Attorney kept lowering the time he wanted me to receive. In two months, they had dropped three years off my time to serve. The next time I went to court, they offered me a three and a half year sentence if I would plead guilty. The lawyer advised me to refuse this offer. The sentence was now reduced to eighteen months. God was with us. I would now only be doing provincial time. Next, they offered me thirteen months. This was incredible! I followed my lawyer's instructions, and we were down to eight months. Now I told the lawyer that I appreciated his help, but I was guilty of those charges, and I would serve the eight month sentence. My lawyer decided to present a letter to the judge. This was a letter that I had written to the police officer who had shot my dog, and whom I had threatened to kill. Shortly after my new life experience with Jesus in Edmonton, I had met with this lady, Pastor Faith, and she helped me compose this letter. I told this policeman how I had my gun aimed at him just after he shot my dog, and how God told me to put it away or I'd die and be forever separated from Him. I knew if I shot him, the other cops would have killed me. I told him because I had listened to God, that he and I were alive today. I told him I was going to turn myself in, and wanted his forgiveness for making this death threat. Vance had Faith give him a copy of this letter before we mailed it to the police officer. Vance had sent the copy of this letter to the lawyer who was now presenting it to the judge.

I received a six month sentence. As a result of the dead time I had already served while waiting to go to court, I had only forty days left to serve. Jesus said that He would be there for me, and He had worked this miracle. I was shipped to Elliot River. I was only there four or five days when the guard needed a fence built. I had done this back at the farm, but I didn't know if I wanted to build prison fences. He explained it was a fence around a fishery outside the prison fences. I asked them for seven dollar a day pay instead of the three dollars, and for a new pair of work boots. I got the job done. This way, I had some money when I left prison. Allan visited me while I was in prison, and picked me up on my release day in February 1997. I got my identification back from the police. Allan took me to the airport and I flew back to Edmonton.

Vance was there to meet me at the Edmonton Airport and gave me a big Christian hug. It was Friday. They wanted me to tell all people at the Mustard Seed Church what had happened to me. I was pleased to do this. It wasn't all about me anymore, but all about Jesus!

Vance got me a job with a farmer with one thousand head of cattle. I lived in a house on the farm. I worked hard feeding and caring for the cattle from sunrise to sunset. I enjoyed the calving season. I was living alone in this farmhouse with no Christian fellowship. I felt I should go back to Vancouver but didn't know why. I heard that voice again, "When you get there, I will tell you where to go." Vance was not sure if this was the voice of God. I wrestled with my decision for two weeks in Edmonton. My money was being used up, so finally, I bought a plane ticket to

Troy Gaglardi, Bill Smith and Bob McGrath

Vancouver. I left with my bag of clothes, and thirty dollars in my pocket. When I arrived at the airport, I told the Holy Spirit that he would have to lead me. I walked and walked from the airport. Eventually, I slept in the entrance of a bank where it was warm and dry. The next day I started walking again. God would lead me to the left, then the right, until I found myself on Carnarvon Street. Then the Lord said to me, "Here!" There were two people coming out of the building, so I said, "What is this place?" The man said that it was a church. The lady said that it was a mission. They asked me if I had come some distance. I told them God had directed me here. They said that I was welcome to come inside. I sat on the sofa. I was so tired. They just let me rest. Then Rob McGrath came and spoke with me. He told me about his life and prison time, and that he was also a child of God. I knew God had led me to this place. He took me in for free that day. He explained that this was Union Gospel Mission, and I was welcome here. It cost $300 a month rent, and $75 for food. I went and got government assistance. The first thing I did was give God my tithe (10% = $50), then paid for my stay, which left me with $75. I really enjoyed working around the Mission helping Kamlesh, Rob's wife, in the kitchen. We would sing to God as we worked. I was able to work with the other men who were living in the house. I got to know Rob very well as he shared more about his life, which was recorded in a book called, Free At Last. After three months, I didn't feel right about living on government money, so sent out some resumes. I went to work grinding the paint lines off the road. It was hard work, but I did a job pleasing to the Lord. I worked my way up from the construction cone "dropper-off", to the cone "picker-up". Eventually, I was the driver of the truck making $1800 a week. We would work nights, and I would always speak to those workers who would drive in the company truck with me. I would tell them about Jesus and about my brother, Rob, at the Mission. They wondered why our last names were not the same. I told them we had different mothers but the same Father (God). I had worked there for two years but none of the men were listening to what I told them about God. Rob suggested that I come work for the House of the Good Shepherd that they had launched. They had five houses to help people get off the streets. I worked with Troy helping with the people at the Royal Oak Residence. One day, Harry, a Christian man, shook my hand, and gave me something. When I found it was money, I gave it back to him, even though he told me it was from God. Rob explained to me later that I should have taken it as God wanted to bless that person who was willing to give to me since I was doing

God's work. There was so much to learn about living God's Way. Sometimes Rob would tell me things, and I would disagree, and I would leave for a while.

One of those times I decided to return to London, Ontario. Every where I went God had some lessons to teach me. I ended up at New Life Centre on Adelaide Street. The pastor that day was the regular pastor's father, Reverend. Karl Thomas, Senior. I really enjoyed the freedom of God's Spirit in this meeting. I started to hang out there. I got to know Pastor Karl Thomas, Jr. I met Michael from the Healing School. The Lord got to 'download' into my soul and mind many truths and scripture verses on how Jesus provided healing of our bodies two thousand years ago when he suffered and died on the Cross.

Next, I went to San Antonio, Texas. It was difficult at first as I slept outside, but the weather was great. Then I delivered flyers for a pizza company and would get paid daily and given a pizza or Chinese food each night. I attended John Hagee's church. I loved going downtown on the Bluebird Buses and bringing people off the streets to the meetings. Pastor Hagee would buy food for them from fast food places. We'd eat our lunch in the park.

After being away from Vancouver for a year, I called Rob from El Paso, and told him all the good things that God had taught me. He met me when I arrived in Vancouver. I went back to the House of Good Shepherd. Rob encouraged me to share the new things that God had taught me. We planned a Healing School at the House of Good Shepherd, which contains a chapel. This Healing School would be for three months, twelve Friday nights. I distributed flyers in the area. A good number came, and I shared the Word of God and how healing and deliverance were all part of the divine plan of God. This lady, Pat, had never been to the House of Good Shepherd, but had seen the flyer in the laundromat. I told people that I didn't need to know their problem, since God did the healing. After the third week, Pat believed the verses from God's Word, went home, and trusting Jesus, received her healing that night. She checked it out. She came back on week four, and although very shy, thanked God for what He had done for her. Another lady, Rosalee, had been a secretary, but had to leave her job as a result her bad back. The specialists didn't know what to do! For five years, it had taken her an hour to get up each morning. After week seven of the Healing School, one morning, she just got out of bed. The next Sunday, at the meeting, she shared a wonderful prayer of thanksgiving. This was all of God and none of me. My righteousness is as filthy rags. If there is any good in me, it is God.

I was then asked to share God's Word at the Healing School at Living Waters Church, then Potter's House. Later, Liberty Life Bible School in Abbotsford, B.C. asked me to teach. They even gave me a title of Professor. I don't get hung up on titles. I guess I was professing the truth of God's Word. I just pray that God will continue to 'download gold nuggets' from His Word, because if He gives it to me, I will teach it and preach it. I have a dream that some day I will be able to get a property in Medicine Hat, and be able to teach at a Healing School. Right now, I remain busy helping those at the House of the Good Shepherd. I am thankful to God who had Rob and Kamlesh meet me on the Mission steps in April 1997. I now want to be there for those in need. Jesus changed me. He can change you. You have to mean it from deep down inside, just like I did, when I prayed for God to get me out of that crack shack in New Westminster. God got me out! God dealt with me individually, and removed all three things that were keeping me from Him. God knows your number, your hang-ups, and your name. He will meet you right where you are! I repented of my sins after hearing God's Word, and Jesus gave me a brand new life, just like it says in the Bible, in 2 Corinthians 5:17. God took care of my problems and He will do the same for you. Now I can answer that question everyone asked me, "Will you ever change your ways?"

I couldn't, I was empty. When I accepted God's gift of forgiveness, and gave Jesus his rightful place in my life, He gave me power to change and make right choices. He continues to change and forgive me daily. Call out to God from deep down inside, doesn't matter where you or what you have done. He can and will deliver you.

Bill Smith
House of The Good Shepherd
7670 Sixth Street
Burnaby, B.C.
V3N 3M7

Chapter Two

CRIME CYCLE

CONQUERED

The Life
of
Cal Maskery

Crime Cycle Conquered!

My dad had violated his parole, now set at eighteen years, and in his paranoia, thought the police were coming for him. He didn't want to go back to prison. He phoned me and told me he was going out West. I told him since I had waited all these years for him, and visited him in prison, that he couldn't just phone and say goodbye. He had to say goodbye in person. He took a cab to my place. Then I told him that I was going with him. He tried to stop me because he would be placing me in danger. The police would be taking no chances with him since he had already shot a policeman. I tried to explain to him how I would feel if he was shot dead by the police. I told him I was going to get a gun and I was going out West with him. I didn't care about my life at this point. I just wanted to be with my dad, as he had shown me love in his own way through the years. I told my dad that he would need me to watch his back. The cab driver was waiting out in the taxi. We went out and got in and went to another part of Scarborough. We got him to stop the taxi. We got him out and told him to get in the trunk of the taxi. He wouldn't get in, so I hit him. My dad told me to stop as we didn't want to hurt him. He got in the trunk. I was only seventeen years old. Another cab driver spotted the cab that I was driving and knew that it was his friend's cab, and that his friend wasn't driving it. He called the police. As I turned onto King Street, downtown Toronto, I saw the police lights behind me. My dad told me to step on the gas. King Street is a very difficult place to have a police chase. I swung onto a one way street – the wrong way. A police cruiser was blocking my escape route. He stepped out of his cruiser with his gun drawn. He saw I wasn't stopping and jumped back just in time and I sped between the cruiser and the parked car. I went down a few more streets, put the taxi into a sideways skid and fishtailed to a stop, and yelled, "Go for it, dad." He ran.

We had become a father and son team. Was I destined to follow in my father's footsteps?

My dad was the son of Donald and Dorothy Maskery and he had four brothers and one sister. My grandfather was a severe alcoholic. My dad, Cliff, grew up in this very troubled and hostile environment. My father had lived in British Columbia since he was four years old, but returned to Ontario as a teenager. He started getting in trouble and had stolen a car during a break and entry and ended up in a training school for a year at the age of fourteen. At sixteen years of age, he met my mother, Margaret Missaube. She was Ojibwa, so my sister and I are half native – First Nations. She was fifteen years old when they started to see each other and went partying together. During that time, my mom conceived me. She was only fifteen. She turned sixteen on February the 7th, 1960. My dad was seventeen years old. They decided to get married since she was now sixteen. They were married on the 4th of March, and I came along on the 14th of March, just ten days later.

I don't remember much about my early childhood. My parents had a very troubled marriage. My father was still drinking, partying, and getting in trouble. He was trying to provide for the family, and decided to do some armed robberies. He did five armed robberies in 1962, and ended up being caught. The police called him the "rifle man" in the newspapers, because he would rob small convenience stores and grocery stores with this rifle. It was winter and the police followed his footprints in the snow to our neighbourhood. They were conducting a door to door search. They were asking questions about my dad's hair. He had dyed his red hair to black, but the red was showing at the roots of his hair. One of the witnesses had noticed this detail. They came to our door and were threatening my mom, so my dad ended up turning himself in to the police. I remember him telling me the story later – how he had felt really bad that on the day of my second birthday, he was sent to Kingston Penitentiary to serve five years for these crimes. It was his son's birthday, and he should be with his son, but he couldn't be there! This first sentence began a life of thirty three and a half years spent in prison for my dad. My sister Laura was three months old when my dad went to prison.

About two years into my dad's prison sentence, my mother met another guy. She was still involved in the life-style of drinking and partying. My dad heard about this in prison, and sent a guy who was on a pass to tell my mother to get rid of this guy or else! This really scared her. She fled during that time to California. When mom and this fellow moved away, I was four years old and my sister was two.

I think my grandfather convinced my mom that we'd be better off with them because of their lifestyle. We moved in with my grandparents on my father's side, and they took on the responsibility of raising my sister and me. I was told my dad was in the army in Kingston, Ontario. I remember visiting my dad in this so-called army. I had many questions as to why there was so much security if my dad was in the army, but then I was young and didn't understand those details. Around the time when my dad found out about my mother and this guy, he escaped from Kingston Pen. He was hiding out in Cobourg, Ontario, and asked his two brothers to come and get him. The police were watching his brothers and followed them. He received additional time for this escape. He was desperate to get transferred out of Kingston so he had a guy stab him in the stomach to force the authorities to transfer him. He was sent to Dorchester Penitentiary, New Brunswick, in the Eastern Provinces of Canada.

I was seven years old when my dad arrived home. He came into my bedroom at 3:00 am in the morning to give me a hug and told me he was home. I was so glad to see my dad. We spent time together and went shopping at the Canadian Tire Store. I also remember him drinking beer with his buddy. I believe he wanted to get his family back together again. He had to get money to go and get his wife back from

California. He met my mother's friend, Eileen, downtown and asked her for my mother's address in California. She would not give him that information but she was willing to dial the phone number if he wanted to speak to her on the phone. They spoke for a while, but she was not willing to come back. He didn't know until much later that my mother was considering coming back to us. He didn't give her time to think it through.

My dad was very impulsive. He decided to commit one more crime to get enough money to fly down to California. Only five days after he arrived home, he and his buddy decided to rob a beer store. My young uncle, who was only sixteen years old, was going to be the driver of the getaway car. They got the money and jumped in the car. The police spotted the getaway car and gave chase. They wouldn't stop, so the police began to shoot through the back window of their car. Finally my dad told my uncle to stop. My dad was afraid my uncle would get shot in the back of the head, and he was just a young boy. The police officers were walking from their car towards my dad's car when my dad opened the passenger door and pulled his gun on the police officer. The police officer pulled his gun on my dad. My dad said, "Don't shoot or I'll shoot." They were standing there with their guns on each other. The other police officer leaned over the hood of the car and shot my dad in the right shoulder. He was holding his gun in his right hand. The trigger was pulled, maybe as a result of being shot, and the police officer in front of him got a bullet in the stomach. As my dad fell from the shot to his shoulder, he dropped his gun. Now my dad's partner got out of the car and was shot twice. The police officer had already fired six shots from his revolver. Now he pointed the gun straight at my dad's chest, as he lay on the ground, to finish him off, but he drew a blank. I thank the Lord that he had used those bullets to shoot through the back window on the car. My uncle jumped out of the car and the police officer spun around and shot him in the elbow. There were eleven shots fired, but nobody was killed. When the police officer went back to the cruiser to radio for help for the fallen police officer, my dad somehow got away and was hiding under a vehicle with his gun. His one arm was useless. They surrounded and arrested him. They were taken to the Don jail to wait for trial.

Dad pleaded temporary insanity and was sent to Penetanguishene, which was designated for the criminally insane at this time. I remember visiting my dad there. It was a horrible place – you would hear blood curdling screams in the middle of your visit. It was scary for me as a little boy. I was 'creeped out' as I walked those corridors. There was an eerie feeling in there. I was getting older now and realized that my dad was not in the army. We were being searched, and going through all these steel doors! I was never told he was in prison. I think I reasoned it out, but continued to play along with them, as it was easier at school to say your dad was in the army.

My Aunt Joy was driving my sister and me up to Penetanguishene to visit my dad when she asked my sister what she wanted to be when she grew up. She responded. Then she asked me what I wanted to be when I grew up. I was only seven years old, but I stated clearly that I wanted to be a bank robber. This freaked her out. She stopped the car and she turned around and said, "Don't ever say that again or you'll get out and walk." I think it triggered all her emotions. She was going to visit her brother who was charged with these serious crimes, and now I wanted to follow in his footsteps.

My dad didn't get the insanity plea and was found fit to stand trial. My dad and his partner were sentenced to twenty eight years in prison – fourteen years for armed robbery and fourteen years for wounding a police officer. My uncle, who was sixteen, didn't get prison time. They took into account my dad's influence over him. Even with time off for good behaviour, it would be years before my dad would be out of prison. We'd visit dad every three months. He'd put his arms around me and say, "Cal, you know I love you." My dad was the greatest guy in the world! I loved his love. I never saw him when he was drinking or on drugs. I didn't see that until much later. He'd be like Jekyll and Hyde. He'd have a total change of personality.

It was during this period of my dad's incarceration that I began to get seriously messed up. Around the age of seven, someone exposed me to sexuality. This is difficult for me to mention, but I have to tell it like it happened. He had me touching him, and other molestation issues began to happen. I remember he was trying to draw me in a little deeper into sexuality. Someone walked in on us one day and was horrified. I felt like I was the one to blame and took on the shame. These experiences opened me up to exploring other sexual issues. We'd experiment at school, and play sexual games, – truth, dare, and double dare – daring each other to do a little more. There were things happening in the school-yard. I got tangled up in this, too. I somehow knew that it was wrong and this compounded my shame and stress. I never talked to anybody about it. I was never taught about sexuality. My grandfather told me superficial things that just made me more curious. I heard things in the schoolyard about boys kissing girls, and so I began to experiment with all kinds of different situations. It never went the way I was told it did for others. I thought there was something wrong with me.

My grandfather was an alcoholic and would always lose his job after a year or two. He was a painter. He also worked in a distillery, and many other jobs. We were always moving. I hated it. Every time I'd go to a new school, I'd just start to make a few friends, and then would have to leave. Every time I'd go to a new school, somebody would give me a push or shove. My grandfather told me to never start a fight. If the fight started, then I was to finish it. This was a lot of pressure for a young boy. I moved to a new school. On the first day of school, a group of us were playing football, and this older boy came and took away our football. I went to get the football and we got into a fight. We came out pretty even. Later, I was told that I shouldn't have messed with John, as he was the toughest guy in grade five. I was scared, but nothing came of it. Then one day I was kicking in the snow, and an ice chip flew across the field and hit John. I saw him give me a hard look. The next moment, I saw him coming towards me with a number of his friends. I was scared, but when he got close to me, I just exploded and got in four or five hard punches. I was amazed at my strength. I earned myself a reputation. I was left alone. When people would bother me, I would just attack and hurt them just like an animal. It was an animal-like reaction that would come over me. I think I allowed some kind of demonic spirit in my life at this time. My sister would tell others not to mess with her or her brother would come after them. Sometimes they would give her a hard time just to get me to fight. I began to get into a lot of fights in the schoolyard. I turned fear into aggression. Everybody thought I wasn't afraid of anybody, yet I was fearful all the time. Nobody knew that I felt this way. I learned to hide my emotions and just be what everybody else expected of me.

I was a clever student. I liked school for that reason. I was good at mathematics and would always work away at it. In grade five, the Gideons, a group of Christian men, came to our school and handed each student a New Testament – a portion of the Bible. I really treasured this gift. It made me feel good. I set it on my dresser, and would read portions of it by the moonlight at night. After my fight with John, my fighting progressed, and I was getting into more trouble at school. It became more difficult to stay focused. At fourteen, I started into smoking, drinking and partying.

I was still visiting my dad every few months. We'd travel to Kingston Penitentiary, Collin's Bay or Joyceville Prison, in the Kingston area. My mom, (my grandmother who I called mom) was not a drinking woman, but she would do anything for her son. She took liquor into the prison. I learned how this could be done. When I was fourteen, I started visiting my dad on my own. He'd ask me to bring in liquor for him. I'd hitchhike to Kingston. I was young, so nobody suspected me. I would hide a mickey in my cowboy boot, and we would drink it during the visit. Then it was two mickeys a visit. I always had a fear we'd get caught. The same fear I had as an eight year old stealing candy from the corner store. I hardened my conscience when I was young. Little things were getting bigger. Then dad asked me to bring him some valium. I would get valium, hash or grass to take to my dad. Soon the quantity of hash or acid increased. When I took dad acid or LSD, he was able to make a profit by distributing it. I would tie it in a plastic bag and carry it into the prison in my body. We learned how to outsmart the officers. Another time, I was driving to see my dad, and was pulled over for speeding. I used one of my uncle's identification, since I was too young for a license. My lies just kept increasing.

My dad got out of prison when I was fifteen years old. He went to a halfway house in Windsor, Ontario. I idolized him. We were drinking and partying. I started to realize there was something wrong with my dad. When he was drinking, he would be a different man. I was alarmed the first time I saw this change! He would become very angry and want to get a gun. He would say, "They'll have to kill me before they take me back to prison. I'll make them shoot me, or I'll take as many as I can as I go." I was fearful, but this was my dad, so I adjusted to this lifestyle. My dad had violated his parole, so the police were looking for him. I stayed in Windsor to cover for him while he returned to Toronto. During this time, my dad and I would just trade girlfriends. If he had a girlfriend, it was okay for me to be with her too. It was a really twisted relationship that began to develop between my dad and myself.

Back in Toronto, my dad ended up meeting with a pastor of a church. This happened because my Uncle Dave came home from a meeting one day and told everyone he had been "born again" (John 3:3). He had confessed his sin, and God had made him his child (John 1:12). I watched with interest as I saw the difference in Dave's life. He was different from the rest of my family. Dave definitely changed. We teased him, mocked him, but he just continued to live the changed life. This Pastor was willing to speak to my dad, even though he was on the run from the police. My dad had a long parole – eighteen years. Later, the Pastor drove dad to Kingston, and dad turned himself in to the authorities.

I asked Dave if I could go to Wallace Memorial Baptist Church with him. I watched the people, and loved to listen to the Pastor preach. When he preached, he was so enthusiastic, and I could see a light around him. (Maybe it was because I was in such darkness?) He would always be at the back of the church and shake my hand. He would take his big hand and put it in mine and say, "Cal, it's so good to have you here. Please come back again." I began going back for that handshake. I'll never forget the effect he had on me. He had such a peace about him. I tried the youth meetings, but didn't seem to fit in. I gradually got away from going to church and back to drinking.

I ended up in the Don Jail one night for stealing my uncle's girlfriend's car. I knew this guy who had been in prison with my dad. He had gone through a sex change, and was working as a prostitute. This man was giving her a hard time. I was angry and confronted him. He was in his car in the alley and I started to punch him through the open car window. Then this prostitute used a brick on his head and knocked him out. The police were coming, so we jumped in the car, her door flew open and the door got crunched. The police had to circle the block, so I managed to get a few streets away and into a parking lot. I was only sixteen years old and thought I was clever to be able to evade the police. We went back an hour later to check things out. The police recognized me. I ended up in jail because charges were laid.

They were dropped since the victim was a married man and didn't want his wife to know he was visiting prostitutes.

I started to evade the police just for the adrenalin rush. When the police would pull me over, I would scheme a way of escape. One time, I cranked the wheel, killed the lights and coasted into the police station parking lot. Another time, I just took a motorcycle for a joyride. I had no helmet and the police were chasing me. I took all the back streets and made it back home safely. My life was out of control.

Suddenly, I got a phone call from my mother in California. I hadn't heard from her in over twelve years. She asked me if I would like to go and live with her. I decided to go since nothing was going well for me in Toronto, and my dad was in prison. She sent me a plane ticket. I looked older, so I swallowed some shots of whiskey on the plane to try and numb my feelings. I didn't know what to expect when I saw my mother after all these years. I had never experienced a mother's love. It was my grandfather who brought my sister and me to their home. My grandmother would look after us on her own while grandfather was out drinking. I felt we were a burden to my grandmother. Now I found out mother's side of the story. She didn't know my grandfather was such a severe alcoholic. It bothered her that we had been raised in this environment when she could have offered us a better home. She was doing well and worked for Pacific Telephone. Ben, her new husband, was a nice guy. We would go out as a family. I started back to school, but I was still messed up. I skipped school and came home with my friend. We were pretty drunk when Ben walked in and asked. "What are you doing, boys?" I was angry. I rose up in front of him and said, "Don't ever call me boy. Only my dad calls me boy." I don't know why I did that because he was really a good man. I had always had this emptiness inside of me not knowing where I belonged. I really wanted to be in a family, but didn't know how to put it all together. After a four month visit, I returned to Canada.

Now I became friends with Terry, one of my uncle's friends. One time when I was high, I told him that next week I was going to church. This shocked him and he asked me why. I told him that I didn't know why, but felt there was something good there. I didn't go, but there was that tug in me that there had to be more to life than the life I was living. Terry smoked a lot of marijuana. I didn't smoke it because it made me paranoid. Alcohol was my major weakness. Now Terry introduced me to the drug 'speed'. He also introduced me to the needle. He showed me how – the vein stuff. He couldn't find a vein in his arm since they had collapsed from overuse, so he put it in his ankle. I don't know if it was the same needle or a different needle, but he put a needle in my arm that night. I remember the feeling that went to my brain. He looked at me and said, "You liked that, didn't you?" I said, "Wow, that's incredible." Then he said, "Don't ever do it again." I asked, "What do you mean?" He said, "You'll kill yourself if you do it for the rush." It put a fear into me. I never ever did another needle again. I began experimenting with other kinds of acid and drugs. Needles would probably have killed me because I was very obsessive in the things I did.

My dad got out of prison on parole. We were in High Park in Toronto. We were laying there drinking and enjoying the afternoon sun. He was telling me about these reincarnations and how we were coming back again in another life. I was getting very depressed with all this. I was having enough problems with this life. All of a sudden, I sat straight up and said, "dad, I don't know how I know this, but we're going to be used in life together for something. There's a purpose for our lives. We're going to be used to do something worthwhile." It was such a positive feeling. That thought was straight from God, but I didn't realize it at the time, but we have both lived to see it happen. I lay back down and went on drinking.

My dad planned to go out West, but that didn't happen! As you have already read, we hijacked a taxi from its owner. The police were informed and gave chase in downtown Toronto. When we ran out of options for escape, I fishtailed the taxi to a stop. My dad fled. He ran between the houses but there was a high wall. They arrested him. Then they discovered the taxi driver in the trunk. I felt really bad. He must have been terrified during the police chase. I was so thankful we didn't crash and hurt that man. I always felt bad about this, even years later. They brought us to the Don Jail. We spent six months together in the Don Jail. This was not a good decision on their part because I was learning to be more like my father. I was there living it up on my dad's reputation. One day my dad and I were down in the bull pen waiting to go to court, and he met the police officer that he shot eleven year earlier. They talked like old buddies. Neither one of them had any hard feelings. I think it was a real healing opportunity for both of them. My dad went to get coffee and someone took his seat. My dad was high on valium and so when the guy didn't give him back his seat, I took him on. Some time later I made bail. My dad was kept in custody awaiting trial.

The day of our trial, I showed up in the courtroom downtown. When they called my dad's name, somebody in the court responded that Cliff Maskery has just escaped custody. I was shocked. Just minutes before they were bringing him through the back corridors to the courtroom. He ended up going to a courtroom upstairs. In a room off of the courtroom, one of the guys told my dad that there was a stairwell that led to the street. The judge was coming up at that time. My dad, just on the spur of the moment took off, knocking over the judge. In the confusion, he bolted down the stairs onto the sidewalk and took a cab to West Toronto. All I knew was my dad had escaped custody, but I didn't find out about how until later. I left the courtroom and went downtown looking for my dad. Then I went to West Toronto and was amazed to see my dad walking down the street. I don't know how I recognized him because he was in disguise with a hood and glasses. I honked and yelled, and he realized it was me, and jumped in the car. We lay low for a few days. My dad put me in touch with a weapons dealer who he had met in prison. My dad sent me out to get one gun. I ordered two 45 magnums. I came back to the motel, since we would not be able to get the guns until the next day. I felt something very bad was going to happen, and that we were going to die. I wanted to leave, but my dad didn't want to go, and kept drinking. We passed out on the bed. There was a bang, and the next thing I knew, I was face down and cuffed behind my back. I was taken into the bathroom and they put me in the bathtub facedown. The police were saying nasty things, and telling me one twitch and they'd shoot me. I was sure that I was in the bathtub so I wouldn't make a big mess to clean up.

My dad was on the bed. As he went to sit up, they knocked him out with one of their weapons. My dad ended up being charged with possessing a gun. I knew he didn't have a gun. My dad told me later that they told him that if I hadn't been there, they would have finished him off. Instead, they took us both back to the Don Jail until we were sentenced.

My lawyer was a real fighter. I got eight months because I was under my father's influence. My dad ended up getting fourteen years. The newspapers read, "Out like a lion, but in like a lamb." He appealed the fourteen years and got it down to nine, so now he was doing forty-two years. I was shipped to Maplehurst Institution and ended up doing over a year for my charges. I didn't like prison and thought I would never go back behind bars again.

I met a young lady, a friend of my sister. We dated for a couple of years. I really wanted to get my life straightened out. She was a good person and helped get me off the drinking. We decided to go out one night. I drank. Some guy followed her into the washroom. I went in and laid a beating on him. I would just explode with anger. She realized quickly that I couldn't be a social drinker. I began working with her uncle. I was a courier for a mail delivery service. I worked fifty hours a week. Then I worked another twenty hours for Pizza Delight on the weekends. I was doing okay financially, but I was using on the side. I was still drinking occasionally. We got to a place where we were going to get married. Then the wedding date got moved up a little sooner and I started getting nervous. I felt I would never make a good husband or father. I thought of my mom and dad and their history of a broken marriage. I also hadn't dealt with my molestation and sexual experimentation. I had a poor self image and I wasn't ready for marriage. I knew I was destroying all the good things in my life but didn't know why. I was unfaithful to her, and sabotaged our friendship. She had gone out with her friend, and a guy was bothering her. She phoned me. Dave and I went down, and she pointed out the guy. I just hit and hit him until he was knocked out. This uncontrollable rage just took over. Then I saw a group of guys making their way to us, so Dave went one way, and I another. Four or five guys tackled me. I don't know if I got stabbed or if I cut my arm on glass, but I was pleased to see the police this time, because everyone scattered. I remember I was taken to court as the guy I beat up was badly hurt. I was sentenced to five months for assault and went back to Maplehurst. When I got out, my girlfriend and I got into a fight and she called the police. They put me in the back seat of the police cruiser handcuffed. She came to the window so I kicked the window, just to show her that I was angry with her. The police officer in the front seat turned around and punched me. Before I knew it, my foot went over the seat and I kicked him. Two or three police officers just pounded me until I was unconscious and brought me to the police station. I got weekend lockups.

I went to visit my Dad in prison and told him I was going out West, to start again in Calgary. He had a bad feeling about me going to Calgary and said that he figured I'd get myself cornered and do something stupid and end up in prison for a long time. I didn't listen this time. Dave and I took the bus. We took some dope to sell to get an apartment. After ten days of partying, the dope was gone, I was missing my former girlfriend, and wanted to return to Toronto.

Dave suggested we could break into a warehouse and get some money. It was supposed to be a simple break and enter, but the owner's son was in the office. We didn't know if he'd called the police, so we tied him up and put him in the back seat of the car and drove out of Calgary. The next morning as we were traveling through Saskatchewan in this man's car, I realized that I was now involved again in kidnapping a person, just as dad and I had done in Toronto. This sick feeling came over me. I didn't know what to do. I was so tired, so we untied our victim, and made him our driver. We told him one wrong move and we'd kill him. He was trying to talk us into letting him go. I knew he would identify us, and I actually considered for the first time in my life about taking someone's life. When I told Dave this, he panicked. I knew I was seriously sick.

We were going through Manitoba and a police car had somebody stopped on the other side of the highway. He was giving this person a ticket. He let him go, and came across four lanes and pulled us over. We weren't speeding. The driver was just answering his questions, and he was checking identification. Then the police opened the driver's door and told him to get out. He let our driver go, and put us in the cruiser. I don't know how he knew what was going on. For a minute, Dave and I were left alone. Dave asked me, "What's our story?" I was tired of lying and conniving. I said, "Tell it like it like it happened." I think that in my heart I was so relieved to be caught. I was happy that the police had stopped me before anything worse had happened. The next day, the police brought us back to Calgary. The front page of the newspaper said, "Police Officer Pulls Car Over On A Gut Instinct."

I was put in Calgary Remand Centre. I was placed

in one of two cells right next to the prison chapel. Though I wouldn't go to Chapel, I would hear the Salvation Army personnel come in each Sunday morning and night. They would bring their musical instruments and the inmates would praise the Lord with them. I could hear it through the walls of my cell. It bothered me that those people were so happy when I felt so miserable. I didn't know that several families in that church in Toronto where I went as a teenager were praying for me all through those years.

Now I began to bargain with God. If you get me a lighter sentence, like less than two years, I would give Him the rest of my life. We made a deal with the lawyer that instead of taking this to high court, we'd save the authorities thousands of dollars by pleading guilty in lower court to break and enter, armed robbery, and kidnapping. There was a deal supposed to be set with the Crown Attorney that if we pleaded guilty, we'd get two, three, or at the most four years. I knew that was a good deal for the second time around for me on a kidnapping charge. This time I wasn't with my dad. We went to the court, and pled guilty, and the Crown Attorney stood up and asked for substantial penitentiary time for us due to our criminal records. My heart just sank. I thought, you can't even trust the justice system. I was sentenced to seven years for kidnapping, four years for armed robbery, and two years for break and enter, which would run concurrent. My last hope was that I'd get to go to Milllhaven Prison to be with my father. We were held at Stony Mountain Prison. I fought another guy so I'd get locked up. It would give me a better reputation, and get me transferred sooner. The warden came down to segregation and told me I was being transferred to Millhaven. Everything was working well. I would be with my father.

I got on the plane peacefully thinking everything was fine. This was a fifty-seater plane. I had shackles around my ankles, and my hands were shackled to my waist. It was a really windy day and I was just deathly afraid that we were going to crash. Fear was coming over me. What if we crash? I can't swim. My hands are buckled to my waist. Questions about my life were just plaguing me. It was the worse experience in my life being in that airplane. As we're coming into the Kingston Airport, my partner, Dave, in route to the bathroom whispered to me, "Cal, we're going to Dorchester." At Kingston, inmates were getting off the plane, but we didn't get off. We were being sent to Dorchester Penitentiary. In the Fall of 1980 a guard was killed there during an escape. A couple of inmates had tried to escape from Dorchester by switching into guard's clothes. A shot was fired by another guard at what he thought was an inmate, but it was actually a fellow guard. I remember hearing about this accident. Now I was going to Dorchester Pen. I was terrified. I was twenty-one years old. The security blanket of having my dad with me had been ripped away. I remember driving up the old road to Dorchester Pen. at 10:00 pm and seeing the towers, the walls, and the guards in the towers. I had this dreadful feeling that I was going to die here. Seven years. I wouldn't make it! The steel door clanged behind me. Knowing there were lots of fights, and people being piped made me realize I was in a fearful place. I began to lift weights and eat regularly. I got involved in the boxing program and worked out on the heavy bag. I built myself up in case it ever came down to a battle. That first year, I kept asking for a transfer back to Millhaven. This was a very lonely time in my life as I had no visits. I felt like I was dying. I'd lock myself in my cell. I was so angry. I blamed the police for taking my father away. I always pictured my father and I shooting it out with the police in front of my family, and making them kill us. My thoughts were out of control. I'd run five miles at night during exercise time, but I couldn't get away from the feelings inside of me. Something was wrong. I felt like I was going to explode. Then I remembered when my dad was desperate for a transfer when he was younger, he got someone to stab him. I decided to force them to transfer me. I knew this guy

Dorchester Prison 1984 before Cal's conversion

who would do it. He was in for stabbing another inmate and for murder. He was a friend of my father's. We planned it perfectly. In prison, if you get stabbed or beaten, often it's because you've been in for a sexual offence, or you've given information to the guards. I didn't want a bad name, so I told three or four solid guys our plan. Once it was all over, they could tell the rest of the inmate population – the grapevine in prison is incredible. This guy stabbed me in the stomach. Another person stabbed Dave in the shoulder. Then they dragged us out and called the guards. It took thirty minutes for the ambulance to come to the prison from Moncton, and thirty minutes to get me back to the hospital. I panicked when I realized what I had done. I could die. I was treated at the hospital and put in a room with a guard to watch me. I hated guards so I demanded to go back to the prison. The doctor gave permission. I went to the prison hospital and then to segregation for four months. I got an infection, but I survived. No transfer happened!

Over the next couple of months there was a Satanist in the prison who tried to get me to give my life to the devil. I just thought about it. I didn't fit in anywhere else. Maybe this was a way I could fit in. He sent me down a satanic ritual. I had it laid out in my cell. There was the five-pointed star and I was looking at the directions for the ritual sacrifice when this voice came over me and said, "Don't do it." It was so strong that I knew I had to listen. I let him know I couldn't do it. He yelled back down to me, "You believe, don't you?" Before I could think, I heard myself saying forcefully, "Yes, I do." When I said that, it shook me. I thought, believe in what? I've got to be believing in God. This really affected me. God used that guy to shake my foundation and make me realize that I had come to believe there was a God.

A few weeks later another guy, a real militant, killer in the prison, in the cell block above me, was talking about how the world was going to end. He mentioned 666 was the number of the antichrist who was going to rise up and pro-claim to be god.

I yelled up to this guy, "How do you know the world's going to end?"

He said, "Well, it's in the Bible."

I said, "Where in the Bible? I went to church as a kid and I never heard anything like that."

56

He said, "Look at the last book of the Bible."

I remembered how the Gideons had put a Bible in all the cells. When I first went in my cell – there was the Bible. I had felt too guilty to throw it in the garbage, so I put it on the shelf out of sight. I pulled it down and I began to read my Bible for the first time since I was a kid. The Book of Revelations fascinated me – all the images, the beast, the demons, and the false prophet. It seemed to be jumping from person to person. So much stuff was happening. It was scary but it was interesting. When I got to Revelation 20, it said that the devil was cast into the lake of fire with the beast and the false prophets. A relief came over me that I didn't give my life to the devil a couple of weeks earlier. I kept reading, and verse 12 told me that everyone whose name was not found written in the book of life would be cast into this lake of fire. It scared me when I realized that meant me. I was not following God. If I died, even though I didn't give my life to the devil, I would end up in the lake of fire with the devil because I was a sinner. I didn't read much more. I put the Bible away.

About this time I received my first visit in sixteen months. My sister, Laura, came all the way from Toronto to see me. I knew there was something wrong. She came to visit me and told me my oldest uncle had committed suicide. It didn't bother me when she told me, but when I went back to my cell it affected me. I wondered where Mark was now. It made me think about life after death. During that visit, she brought some stuff for me into the prison. I smoked it and I went through the most paranoid experience in my life. My heart rate doubled. I was shaking. I was taken to the prison hospital. I was afraid for my life, and called on God to help me. Later, I thought about taking a guard hostage in my cell, to get a transfer, but had no guarantee of a transfer to Millhaven. I could be sent to Quebec, Alberta, or British Columbia. Then, I thought, maybe I'll just end my life. My uncle Mark had. That night was one the darkest in my life.

The only thing that was stopping me was I was afraid where I would go after death.

As all these thoughts were going through my mind, I looked up at the TV. We only had a TV fixed up on a screen outside in our cell block. We could watch it through the bars. Evangelist Billy Graham was on TV. My grandmother had watched him. I did not listen to him because I felt condemned enough already, and he'd just tell me I was a sinner. My grandfather had preached at me all of my life. He had an excessive view of hell. He used it to lay a guilt trip on us to make us do what he said. I wasn't going to listen to this man on the TV, but this little voice said, "just listen. What do have to lose?" I put the headphones on and for the first time in my life heard the Gospel of Christ. He talked about how God loved us so much that He sent His only son Jesus Christ from Heaven to become a man. He came to live without sin, and die on behalf of sinners to give us a new life. When he was talking about what Christ had done for us, I think in my own criminal mentality, God got a hold of me. I knew from experience that if two or three guys were caught in a crime, then often the one who was facing the longest sentence would make a deal with his buddies to get them off. He was setting himself up to be a hero in the prison system for being solid. There is a sacrificial system, a sacrificial lamb, among convicts, but only because one is going to be sentenced anyway, not out of love. Billy Graham explained that's why Jesus Christ came from heaven to die in my place. He came to sacrifice for me. It really began to penetrate that Jesus did this out of love, and he wasn't guilty. I was beginning to understand the gospel for the first time. I had heard it as a youth in my uncle's church but didn't grasp it then.

I didn't respond to the message that night, but it kept replaying in my mind. Three or four days went by. I wasn't sleeping properly, I was just thinking about it. On the fourth night, I knelt down by my bed and said, "God, if you are really out there, please come into my life." I made God a promise that if he would make himself real to me, then I would give him the rest of my life. Nothing happened that night, except somehow in my gut, I just knew that if there was a God, He had heard my prayer. I went to bed and awoke the next morning filled with this amazing peace. The anger, fear, and emptiness were gone. I didn't know how to describe it because I had never experienced this feeling at any time in my life. I laid there for eight to ten minutes wondering, then I suddenly remembered my prayer. I knew He was making Himself real to me. I sat up in bed, and said, "God, if this is really what it's all about, then I want all that you are inside of me." I began to give Him all areas of my broken life. The fact that my mother left when I was a young child, and my dad was always in prison had left me with major abandonment issues. I remember saying to God, "God, if you will never leave me, I will live for you all of my days." Later, I read from the Bible, "I will never leave you nor forsake you." I also read "when your mother forgets you, I will never forget you." I was finally home – a child in God's family. This brought such peace and excitement to me. I grabbed the Bible off the shelf and started to read it.

I didn't know where to start. I wrote my Aunt Joy who had come to the Lord shortly after my Uncle Dave. She had been on her way to becoming an alcoholic but had cried out to God, and God delivered her. She attended that church where my uncle Dave was going and somehow married the minister's son. She was so excited that I had given my life to Jesus. She wrote back, sent me booklets, and told me to read the Gospel of John. I went to look for this book in the Bible and found four Johns. The Gospel of John with twenty chapters, and there were these three little books of John near the end of the Bible. I thought she must mean these little ones. She wouldn't start me off on a big book. I went to the little books. When I got to 1st John 2, verse 27, it talked about "the anointing which we have received from Him abides in us, and we need not that any man should teach us." I wrote my

Aunt Joy and told her I had been reading these three gospels of John and I had a lot of questions. Joy's husband started to write and explain things to me. Joy then told me to read the Gospel of John with twenty chapters. I found this much easier to understand and it told me more about Jesus. I believe God had me read those little books first for a reason, because I was wondering who could pastor me and how could I grow and be trained, since I was in prison. God wanted me to know the anointing of the Holy Spirit on his Word – the Bible – that it was the answer. God was going to be my teacher. As I read stories of the healings and the miracles of Jesus, I got so excited and wondered why I had never heard these things? I probably did, but I had walked away, blinded by the devil. I kept reading and got to the evening of Jesus' death. The night before he spent time with his disciples. Five chapters – John 13 to 17 give the details. It told how He's going back to Heaven to the Father and the Holy Spirit would come and be our Comforter. As I read about that Comforter, for some reason, it just struck me in my heart. I realized that was what I had been looking for all my life, to be comforted. I was drinking, doing drugs, and was into unhealthy sexual relationships looking for something to fill the emptiness in my life, but nothing satisfied. Suddenly, my mind was opened up as I knew that this Comforter, which Jesus had asked the Father for, was coming into my life. He was the anointing that I had read about that would lead, teach and guide me. I was so excited, tears were rolling down my cheeks. I had turned tears off years ago. Now these hot tears were coming down my cheeks, I just felt so loved. I felt a presence with me, it was so real. I threw my arms open wide and said, "Lord, take over my life. Make me whatever you want me to be. I want to be a blessing and to help people." I read the Bible night after night. I was so excited in my faith. I wrote my aunt and told her about the changes in my life.

Then I had this feeling – this deep desire that I should be telling my father about my faith in Jesus. I didn't want to write him. I thought my father would be ashamed of me. Here I was, his son bringing drugs into the prison and now I was a religious person. I knew I wasn't religious. It wasn't religion. I had found a friend. He was my God and my friend at the same time. I knew he wouldn't understand it that way. I just somehow couldn't bring myself to tell him. A week, then ten days went by, and this feeling was still there – to write my father. I just couldn't hold back anymore, so I sat down and wrote – Dad, I've got to tell you what's happened to me. I've given my life to Jesus Christ and I'm going to walk with Him for the rest of my life. That was all I wrote as I didn't have much more to say. I didn't expect him to answer me. I signed and sent it. There was no answer. After I wrote him the first letter, something freed me to just write him. I told him to try Jesus. I told him I was not talking about religion or church, but the person, Jesus Christ, and how He could to come into his life. I used the court system to tell my dad about Jesus. I would write things like – God is like the judge in the courtroom and Jesus is our lawyer who is there on our behalf. He's fighting for us. The Crown Attorney is like the devil and he's there to condemn us, tell all the evil things we've done, and get us locked up. I explained how Jesus was not only our lawyer, but also paid the penalty for our crimes. He was also our sacrifice. He did our 'time' for us. I was using the court system to tell my dad about Jesus. Meanwhile, I was praying to God that whatever it took to save my father, to please do it. Shake him up, turn him over, flip him backwards, but please make yourself real to him. I started to pray that God would not let Satan kill my dad. There was a real urgency that my dad was going to die. He was just going to kill himself, or get himself killed.

Two and a half months went by and no letter came from my father. I wasn't surprised because I knew he wouldn't process this well. I knew in his mind it would be an end of me bringing him stuff, and an end to our partnership in crime. I kept praying for him daily. Finally, it happened!

He told me years later. After three months, dad replied, "Cal, I have seen such a change in you through your letters. I've given my heart to the Lord." I was so excited. My next thought was "No, this can't be. My dad thinks I'm giving him a tip on how to get out of prison early." Some guys do use the Chapel. They tell their parole officers they go to Chapel and do the programs. They do the Chapel thing, and get out and do their own thing in their own strength, and are back in prison in a few weeks or months. I thought now my Dad is going to use the Chapel.

Then I got a letter and he told me about the joy and the peace that he had found. He told me that the Holy Spirit had come into his life and that he was free. For some reason, when he said the Holy Spirit, I knew that he had had an encounter with the Lord. My mind went back through the years to bars and nightclubs where we'd curse Jesus and God, but nobody talked badly about the Holy Spirit. I got so excited. I felt I was exploding with joy. My dad was saved, my dad believed! I began to run around the prison telling people my dad had given his life to Jesus. Dave started to listen now. He knew my dad from prison. He would always tell me that I could go to Chapel, but he was going to the gym.

My dad told me what happened years later when I finally got out of prison and went to visit him. There was an argument in the kitchen at Millhaven. That night, this guy returned to the cell block all pilled up, with four of his buddies. When the cells were opened and before my dad knew what had happened, the first guy jumped into the cell with a baseball bat and split my dad's head wide open. As he was coming down again with the bat, my dad grabbed the bat. He knew he couldn't let himself get knocked out, or he'd be killed. My dad was still reeling from that first blow when the other two guys jumped into the cell with the bars from the dumbbell from the weight pit. They were hitting him over the back of the head with these short steel bars. The fourth guy finally jumps in the cell. My dad's arms were over his head holding the bat, and dad was just waiting for the fourth guy to bury a shank in his heart. My dad told me he watched his eyes, and he froze for a moment. He hesitated to plunge the knife. In that moment my dad got the bat off the other man. They all fled. He ended up in the hospital in pretty rough shape. They stitched him up. He spent a number of weeks in the hospital. There was a Bible there. My letters were still coming to him. Dad, try Jesus. It's not religion, it's Jesus Christ. Finally he said, "Jesus, I've seen the change in my son, and if you can do this in my life too, I'm giving you the rest of my life. I'm giving you one more chance to make yourself real to me." What he meant by this was that he had tried twice to connect with God. He didn't understand that he needed to call on Jesus. My courtroom scene had helped him understand how Jesus' shed blood allows us to come to God. This time when he prayed he was desperate, and God started to changed his life, and is doing that to this day, even as He is changing each of our lives.

Dave, challenged by my change, and now my father's change of heart, opened the New Testament. I told him to read from Matthew 24. Here he read about the return of Jesus and how Jesus was coming back for the believers. He told me as he was reading he realized that my dad and I would be going to heaven because we believed, but that he would be left behind. He didn't want that to happen so he prayed and believed, and Jesus changed his life. When my dad and then Dave gave his life to the Lord, something happened inside of me. I just began to be aggressive. I started going out in the prison yard and telling people about Jesus. I thought they'd see the change in my life, my dad's and Dave's life, and want it. Some of them would cross the yard when they saw me coming. I wanted everyone to experience this joy and peace. Within a few months, I realized I could not force people. God began to teach me to just share with them and let God work in their hearts.

I'd go to the Chapel and listen to teachers like

Charles Taylor. He was an educated man from Acadian Divinity College in Wolfville, Nova Scotia. He'd come into the prison and do workshops with us. Reverend Pierre Allard, who was the Chaplain, would bring in volunteers from the community. There was this girl who was coming in that was going to the Atlantic Baptist College in Moncton, New Brunswick. She grew up in a religious home and knew about the Bible, but had never had a personal experience with Christ. She went off to Bible College. During her time there, she was invited to a Leighton Ford Crusade, who was an associate of Billy Graham's. When the invitation was given at the end of the service, she made her decision to personally accept Christ. She didn't know why she went forward, because she had believed in God all her life, but she knew there was an emptiness in her life. She asked Jesus to make Himself real to her and forgive her personal sins. She didn't really feel anything. She went home that night, read her Bible out of habit, but this night, the words were alive – 'leaping off the page'. Jesus was becoming real to her. She was born into God's family. She came into the prison as an expression of her faith and part of her practical training for Bible College. The volunteers were all trained not to have personal contact with the inmates. We met at one of Charles Taylor's workshops. At the end of the group sharing session, everybody was asked to share two things about their life. I was terrified. I had never shared about my life. They took a break and as Rose walked by me, she mentioned that God had spoken to her through this group. I asked her how she knew God spoke to her. She said that through some of the things that were shared, God had given her a better understanding of what was happening in the men's lives. This helped her to be more sensitive to their needs. It fascinated me that God would speak to individuals. I had this voice inside of me that would tell me to do things, but still I hadn't clued in that it was God who was speaking to me.

After a couple of months I began to really care for

Rose. The next time I went to Chapel she was sitting with a couple of friends, but she came over to me. I realized she too had an interest in me. Finally, I asked her to come and visit me in the visiting room. We were both nervous. I didn't know how to talk to a girl. It had always been sexual. I took her hand and prayed, "God, please help us to communicate and show us where to start." We talked about the Lord and different things. Three hours went by so quickly. We arranged for another visit. We'd talk about our lives. Eventually, she was asked to make a decision whether she was going to come to the Chapel or continue to visit me. She couldn't do both according to the prison regulations. She prayed about it and decided that she'd continue to visit me. She visited me for the next three years until I was released.

I went through a real time of soul searching. This verse kept coming to me, "confess your sins one to another, pray one for another and you will be healed" (James 5:15), I just couldn't understand why I had to do this. That voice inside me told me to tell her about my past. I thought she would walk away when she knew about my ugly past. Then I decided that if I was going to marry this girl one day, she needed to know where I had come from. I started out by telling her about the molestation. She would tell me that I was a new creation, and old things were passed away (2 Corinthians 5: 17). It was harder to tell her the other things that happened which were not done to me, but that I had done to others. I was amazed that she could see me for who I was becoming in Christ and that the past was gone. The more I shared and didn't bury these issues the more I knew I was accepted in Christ. I reckon myself dead to those issues, and alive to God. It was like weights coming off of me as I confessed. God was healing me.

One day I went to another inmate who had been a believing Christian for a year longer than me. I told him I was having problems forgiving myself. He looked at me and he put his finger up toward my chest and said, "Who are you little man, not to forgive yourself, when God Almighty sent His Son for you?" My first reaction was, "Who is he calling a little man?" Then it hit me. Here I am, just a piece of dust on the earth, looking up at a big Creator, thinking He cannot forgive me? Jesus had paid the penalty on the Cross. I didn't need to carry it. If I didn't believe then I was making His sacrifice for no purpose. This freed me from years of torment.

I'd go up to the Chapel and volunteers would come in and put their arms around me and tell me they loved me. Elsie was in her late fifties. Her husband had died in an accident and she had raised eight children. She just came to love and care for us. I learned what the Bible meant about God giving us families. Elsie became my spiritual mother. After I was released, Elsie welcomed me in her home. This meant so much to me.

That voice inside me was telling me that I had something to give the world that Jesus could not give them. I thought that was arrogant, so I asked Him what it was. He brought this thought to me that Jesus was without sin so had not experienced sin. I had experienced sin, so I could help those who had fallen, by telling my story. He wanted me to live my life as an open book and share with others, what God had brought me out of, even about the sexual deviations. It was difficult but I knew if I was obedient that it could bring freedom through Christ to others.

Rose was walking through Victoria Park in Moncton and God told her I was going to be a preacher. This was no coincidence because just a couple of weeks earlier, I had asked God what I was to do with my life. Then I was out in the prison yard, and I felt I should speak to this man who was walking in the yard. Three times he came around the yard, and finally, I obeyed. He told me that God had told him to speak to me, and he was wondering how to approach me. Then he gave me the message God had given him for me that I was going to be a preacher. This was another confirmation about what God was speaking into my heart. I decided to use my 'time' to get to know God's Book. God arranged that Frank and I would work in the same area and we were able to encourage each other in God.

Time came to prepare for parole, and I told them about my life change, but they didn't believe it as they had heard that same story a thousand times. Parole was denied. It didn't bother me. God had His reason. The guards and inmates knew that I was different.

I got an opportunity for a written parole, but my request was denied. I was at peace. I felt like Paul, the Apostle, who was sent into Arabia for three years before his time of ministry. God began to deal with me about some charges I needed to clear. I was guilty, and had them brought into Moncton. The day I went to court, I asked God to be with me. As I stepped between the double gates that led to outside and the paddy wagon, a deep peace enveloped me. God gave me the words to speak in that hour, just like He promised. I was sentenced, but all three sentences ran concurrent, and so I didn't have to serve additional time, and my record was cleared. As I stepped back inside the prison gates, that deep peace lifted.

When I asked Rose to marry me, she prayed and God told her to wait. Christians were cautioning her. I sincerely understood that they were protecting her. Finally, I was to be paroled to Toronto. I was released to a halfway house in Moncton. Now we were to be married. I asked Gerry Bezanson to be my best man. He was a Christian serving a life sentence for a crime that happened before his New Life experience. He applied for a pass, but was denied. It was a week before the wedding and everyone wanted me to get a backup best man. I believed, and three days before the wedding, without an appeal, Ottawa overturned its decision. The Christian community, all one hundred and fifty believers, gave us a beautiful wedding. A former guard, now Chaplain Garry Porter, gave me the keys to his car to drive to our motel

Maskery Family

outside of Moncton. We flew the next day to Toronto to my Aunt Joy and Uncle Rob's in Pickering, Ontario. Later, we found an apartment. God gave me a job working at Mitchell Family Bookstore. I was selling Bibles, books, and gospel music. I would tell my story to customers. After eighteen months, I became restless as I didn't get any opportunities to share with people who needed to hear what God had done for me.

We returned to Moncton, and when Nathan was born, I lifted him in my arms, and dedicated him to God. (I dedicated each of my children in the same way, as each child

68

is a gift from God.) I became a house painter and had many opportunities to tell my story. After three years, Gloria, called to tell me Dan had been killed on Highway 401. I visited her in Peterborough, Ontario, and she gave me three cheques for the next three months for my Ministry. When I returned to Moncton, I was approached to become Director of New Life Mission. What started as a Children's Ministry, eight years later, had become an Adult Outreach. We were talking to people on the streets, and in nightclubs. We were holding Bible studies, and I was constantly ministering to people. My marriage was suffering, but God placed people in my life to counsel me, and we learned how to work together.

The mission grew into a church which we called Shekinah Christian Fellowship. (Shekinah means glory of God). We remained interdenominational, just bringing people to Christ as Saviour. I still felt a tug to be on the cutting edge for those living on the fringe of society, and so we rented a storefront. We had pool tables, dart boards, and a coffee lounge. Someone suggested "Harvest House" and the title stayed as we were bringing in His Harvest. The first Harvest House started in 1997. Arthur started renting rooms at this place on Mountain Road. God brought in people like Gerald. He was white as a ghost, skinny, and lived on a park bench, but we gave him a room. He would come to the Drop In Centre during the day, and he found the love of Jesus. He is still working with us nine years later. Another fellow, Robert from Cape Breton, was coming to kill the person who had violated him. He was so high on cocaine when we met him, but after telling him about Jesus, and a simple prayer, he was totally set free. In a moment, all his sin and desire for drugs were gone. I began to realize God deals differently in people's lives. Robert was changed in a moment, but Gerald took two weeks to come out of the fog after twenty years of cocaine addiction.

In 1998, Tony, who was servicing the Esso's in Prince Edward Island, suggested I needed a break. So once a month I would take this two day trip with him. He introduced me to Bev. God changed her life, and the next month she had friends who wanted to speak with us. God was changing more lives, and so we rented a room next to the soup kitchen in the Basilica. When it became too small, we moved to a storefront. God provided the rent each month. This outreach was costly due to the bridge crossing. It was time consuming as it was a two hour drive from Moncton. God was giving us time to train workers. Noel received a passion for this work. We have watched as God has grown this Harvest House in Charlottetown under his leadership.

Next was North Sydney, in Cape Breton! It was a five to six hour drive from Moncton. The ferry for Newfoundland leaves from here. Lily spoke with me and offered to move there if we opened an outreach. I was about to do this when a number of people suggested I wait. I didn't understand, but listened to their counsel. God had his purpose. I came home one night and I had received an e-mail from Arizona. This person typed in Cal Maskery, and information on Harvest House was displayed. It was my mother, who I had not seen in twenty-four years. With financial help from the Christians, Rose and I, and our children, Nathan, Alisha, and Kayla, drove to Arizona and spent two to three weeks with Mom. We really got to know each other. She couldn't believe the change from a sixteen year old alcoholic teenager to a man with a Mission in the Maritimes. She went to church with us a number of times. God was moving on her heart. Later, she attended church and asked for prayer as she was scheduled for heart surgery. People prayed and she felt God's presence. After further examination, it was decided she didn't need surgery as God had healed her. She asked Jesus to change her life, and forgive her sins. God had answered my prayers for my parents that I had prayed from prison many years earlier.

Randy, and my son, Nathan, went with me on my next trip to North Sydney. The women in Prince Edward

Island had given us a collection of finances – enough for the first month's rent. We found a place and opened. People said we wouldn't last six months, but we are there to this day because God sent us there, to reach out with the love of Jesus. God gave us faithful volunteers. About six weeks later on our trip, Randy wanted me to read this book, The Prayer of Jabez. I had to read it out loud as we travelled. It was about enlarging our territory. On our return trip, I told Randy that we should check out Glace Bay, Nova Scotia. He agreed.

The next time, Randy, Lily and I made the trip, and we stopped in Glace Bay. We saw a Youth Centre but it was boarded up. We found the owner, Roy, but he wanted $600 plus utilities. We were just getting North Sydney started, and we were moving out of our comfort zone, but we asked to see the building. He opened the doors and it had coin operated pool tables and a canteen. Wow! He asked us about our plans. We told him we were a Christian organization that helped those getting off drinking and drugs, and providing a place for them to stay until they got established. He pointed at me, and said that if we would use it for this purpose then we could have the building. I asked if he believed in God. He told me he believed in someone, but not the church. Melvin had been traveling with us and helped with renovations. As we watched him mingling with those at the outreach, we knew in our spirit that Melvin was the man for this outreach. At first Melvin and Hazel were hesitant, but God enlarged their borders.

God continued to enlarge our borders, and He enabled us to open an outreach and residence in Summerside, Prince Edward Island under the leadership of Chris Blaquire. He provided leadership for the Windsor, Nova Scotia outreach through Blaine and Donna Eldridge. Adam and Alyshia Rice took on the leadership of the new outreach in Sheet Harbour, Nova Scotia.

Lives continue to be changed. One time, a couple came and wanted a place to stay. They were not married, and so were delegated to different rooms. They decided they wanted to get married. We counselled them about God's love and purpose for their lives, and they wanted to follow Him. They knew about God in earlier years. They got their marriage license on Monday. We went to the Bible Camp on Tuesday. I spoke on John 2 about the Marriage in Cana, and then they were married. They also wanted to be baptized, so I took them to the swimming pool on the campgrounds, which was right outside the chapel doors, and baptized them in water. They were so excited, in twenty hours, they were saved, baptized, and married. We saw them off on the boat to Newfoundland at 3:30 am. They are still living for God in Newfoundland.

During this time Claudette Bradshaw, one of our politicians mentioned that $753 million had been raised for the homeless across Canada. We presented what we were doing for the homeless. They purchased a duplex for women in Moncton and another for women in Charlottetown.

One day, I was coming from visiting at Dorchester Prison and God spoke to me and asked if I would be willing to step back from the front lines. Naturally, I agreed. God gave me this vision of a row of soldiers ready to go to battle but each had a problem with their metal armour. I fixed their armour before I sent them out. For ten years, I had been working with people on the streets, now God wanted me to train others to do this work. We started a one year school – Harvest School of Ministry. Many people came, mostly the young. Then God moved me to the next stage. He reminded me of a truck that we had been given two years earlier. The sides folded down into a stage. We started to take youth mission teams trained in drama, skit, and rap to share the gospel in various towns. We worked with the local churches. These 'Ignite Teams' were setting on fire the love of Jesus in people's lives. They would set up BBQ's, or minister in parking lots and parks. God blessed and now we have a number of teams going out each summer.

Then I observed that in some of our resident out-reaches, we would have to ask some to leave because of their addictions. They were pulling others down due to the fact that they were continuing to use drugs. It broke my heart. God started to speak to me about a Recovery Centre. I could not see doing this as we were $50,000 behind in bills at the Moncton Residence. I asked God to confirm His direction to me by clearing this debt by the end of the year which was only ten weeks away. On November 2, 2005, Harvest House Men's Residence in Moncton, caught fire, and there was thousands of dollars of damage. What the devil meant for evil, God turned for good. Radio, and local and national T.V. told our story. Caring people gave and by February 2006, we were operating a separate second floor for drug recovery based on Christian principles at our Moncton Residence.

I was travelling up to Digby, Nova Scotia and passed this sign for a Christian Centre. God had me meet with Eleanor. She is a widow and the place has been empty for twelve years. The directors gave us the property and God sent in teams to help renovate the property. In April 2006, we moved our Recovery Centre and School of Mission to this property. It has proven to be a great mix with dedicated Christians encouraging those coming off addictions. The spiritual program helps the addict address core problems of abuse that often launched them into addiction to cover the pain.

Conrad (Willard) Green, a former biker and drug dealer from Grand Manan is now Coordinator at the Digby Recovery Centre. It is wonderful to see these lives that the devil once destroyed, being restored, and coming to their full potential in Christ.

Dwight and Charmaine, a wonderful couple from Grand Manan Island, gathered together a group of fishermen, carpenters, and mechanics to come and shingle the roof on the Digby Recovery Centre. God ignited their hearts for their home area. A short time later I was invited to visit Grand Manan. A fisherman and his wife offered us a Restaurant

Rose and Cal Maskery

Games Room for an outreach centre for this community. The Village Council offered us the old "Castalia School House" for residential living accommodations. This fall – my son, Nathan, and his wife, Vicky, will be moving to Grand Manan to launch this outreach. The future is God's!

Remember that 'flash experience' I had in High Park, Toronto, as a teenager when I was drinking with my dad? We have both lived to see that fulfilled. My dad, Cliff, now works in the Harvest House Residence in Moncton. We are working together for a worthwhile purpose because of

Jesus. My son and daughters are involved with the Ignite Youth Teams. God has broken the cycle of crime!

I share my story to encourage you to invite Jesus into your life. He'll deal with each of you individually and deliver you from drugs, alcohol, and even those secret sins. Forgive yourself – Jesus paid the price for your forgiveness! Let Him fill that empty void inside of you with His Power. God has taken me on an adventure of faith since I made that promise to him back in 1982. Hand over control of your life to Jesus. He has a bright future for you.

Cal Maskery -www.hhoutreach.org
Harvest House Moncton
P.O. Box 1774
Moncton, New Brunswick
E1C 9X6

Peter Doucette – 25 years (picture of him drinking)

Chapter Three

Abandoned,

Alcoholic,

Authentic!

The life Story
of
Peter Doucette

Abandoned, Alcoholic, Authentic!

I was just five years old when something dreadful happened. Mrs. B. my kind of adopted mom, was sitting in her rocking chair, and all of a sudden fell forward and landed on the floor. I was afraid, and ran to get Betty, my kind of adopted sister. Betty ran to the neighbours. I remember them coming in our house. They confirmed that Mrs. B had dropped dead in front of me. They notified her son who lived in town. The funeral was held in another part of town. After she was buried, one of her sons kind of adopted me. He inherited the house, and I came with the package. I was never legally adopted. Who was I – where did I belong? It would take some years before I would discover the truth.

My mother, Irene, married John. This marriage was failing and so they separated. John had been gone for five years, when my mother met Norman. He was a married man. My mother ended up getting pregnant. I was born in the hospital in Campbellton, New Brunswick, in Eastern Canada on June 24, 1952. There was an elderly woman, Mrs. B. she was about seventy-five years old, who maybe felt sorry for me, or for my mother and her predicament, so took me home from the hospital. She kind of adopted me.

My biological father followed in the steps of his father and wandered back and forth to Ontario throughout his lifetime. Norman's father, Edgar, told my grandmother that he was going to Ontario to find a job. He didn't return for twenty years. My biological father, the next generation, following my conception, was constantly on the move.

Mrs. B. was a tough old woman. In the 1950's she ran a bootlegging house selling booze to the drunks. She also knew how to control them when they got aggressive and nasty. As I grew up in this home, I found out that this woman had also adopted a girl, whom we will call, Betty. She was eleven years older than me. The house was on the west side of town, in an area known as Vinegar Hill, close to a village called Little Montreal. This house was built in the 1800's. It was in a poor area, in what we called a tar-paper community. We burnt coal, wood, and old tires, to keep us warm. We used car oil or fuel to start the fires. We had to survive those cold harsh winters!

Betty was sixteen years old when Mrs. B. died. She married just a short while after her death and moved to Quebec. I found out, when I was an adult, from neighbours, that this woman had prostituted Betty, as a young girl. I remember seeing Betty one more time when I was eight years old when she came to visit Campbellton. She ended up having twelve children. She died in her early 50's in Quebec. One of her daughters made contact with me a few years ago and told me how Betty would often talk about me, little Peter, her adopted brother, with her husband. She had a rough life. I often wonder how she handled all the sexual abuse she suffered.

Mrs. B's son now became my new adopted father. He had a son and two daughters of his own. I believe the old woman loved me and was pretty good to me, but now at her son's home, I was the one who did the chores. I did the splitting of the wood, the kindling for the fire, the hauling of the coal in those old coal buckets. Everything that needed to be done, and no one else wanted to do it, I got to do it. I was the errand boy. Just give it to Peter, he'll do it. I noticed other children in our house didn't have to do all these things. If I did something they didn't like, then they told me that I was stupid and miserable. After years of these messages playing in my head, I lived with the fear of saying or doing something wrong. These messages of rejection came in many different ways. I couldn't go near the refrigerator when I was hungry like the children of this family. I had to wait to be told to sit down and eat. When my step parents would talk to me about any subject they seemed to force themselves into a make-believe conversation that wouldn't last too long. I had no one to listen or really talk with me. I was getting older and had a lot of questions. I was a dreamer, and thought things would get better, but instead a nightmare was unfolding.

There was always a lot of drinking going on in this house too. There was always more drinking on the weekends. I grew up in an atmosphere of fear. I never knew what might happen to me. I never felt wanted or good enough. I was told so many times and in so many different ways how they had taken me into their home. There was no physical abuse, but mentally and emotionally – that was something else! I wasn't allowed to say how I felt. I felt trapped, but too young to run away. I wanted to leave so badly, but there was nowhere to go. I couldn't wait to get older. I had no choice but to hold my hurts inside me. I wanted to be somebody. It seemed like everyone else around me was somebody. I knew there was something missing. The only little bit of happiness would come on the weekends. I knew there would be more drinking with friends and relatives, and things would be more relaxed, and the atmosphere would change, and become more tolerable, even a little friendly.

They had also taken in an old man, George, and he must have been close to eighty years old. We shared a room. He would pay his board, and spend the balance on booze. He would give me a drink. He started me on alcohol when I was ten years old. I soon learnt that on weekends I could sneak booze from the family, and go and hide, and drink it alone or with a friend.

On Sundays, I was expected to go to church. They really didn't believe in it. They were religious people, but not godly people. They were too busy enjoying their drinking to take attending church seriously.

All too soon, I couldn't wait to get my next drink. I was becoming alcohol dependent. It got hold of me real young. Life was forced on me. I was growing up bitter. I said, "Someday I'll get even!" Well, I did get even, or so I thought, but all I was doing was sacrificing me. I had a spirit of revenge. Any time I had a chance to do wrong, to strike directly or indirectly, without getting caught, I would do it.

I was never taught to receive or give anything worthwhile. I had to buy my own clothes. I started selling newspapers when I was about eleven or twelve years old. I had a good size paper route. I got this route from a neighbour because I worked it for him for some time. I missed a lot of time at school, especially when two different newspapers would need to be delivered to over 250 houses. I didn't hate school. I just wanted things that others enjoyed, nice things, and needed finances to buy them. I started to hang around guys older than myself. I started doing break and entries into commercial properties in the summer of 1966.

In September I was arrested, sentenced and transferred to Kingsclear Reform School on October 3, 1966, due to my summer's long list of B & E's. Here I learned more negatives than positives. I found that most of us boys there had broken or twisted lives. I was fourteen. I worked hard to get out of there. I didn't like the place. Sad to say, it was sort of a relief from the home where I had been living. Reform School didn't reform me. After nine months I was released, July 1, 1967. I was given a parole officer. He told me I was an alcoholic. I was only fifteen. He suggested I attend AA (Alcoholic Anonymous). I told him that I couldn't go there, because those were all grown-up men. So I just kept drinking and stealing.

When I was old enough to get my own identification papers, I wrote to Fredericton, the province's capital. There was nothing under Peter Charles Fugere. A name I had used for a while. I did more research, and found that I had been baptized Joseph Peter Parent. This was my mother's married name at the time of my birth. I had gone to school as Peter Joseph B.... I had lots of information, but belonged nowhere.

I went for an interview for a job at a local bar after

my release from reform school. The manager asked if I stole. I thought maybe someone had told him about me being in reform school. It wasn't that at all. He told me that if I didn't steal, then I was no good. He told me that everybody who worked at this bar was a thief. I didn't laugh. I knew what he was talking about. I got the job, and went to work on stealing. I would steal cases of 24 beers and bottles of hard liquor by taking them out at night next to the garbage can. My responsibilities were to clean and restock the bar. This gave me all kinds of opportunities. I was now sixteen and stealing alcohol to supply my needs, not just my alcohol needs, but to medicate my inner needs of fear, hate, rejection, and lack of self worth. I was going to become somebody someday.

I decided now that I was sixteen I should go to the local dances. I met Talbert at one of those dances. He was from Restigouche, now known as Listiguj Reservation. This reservation was across the river from Campbellton, New Brunswick. Talbert and I became drinking buddies. He introduced me to lots of the guys my age who were from the reserve. We would usually end up going to Campbellton, and then we'd go to the bootleggers on Hillside Street. Sometimes there would be twenty to twenty-five of us drinking there. We drank beer, and then bought wine for $2 a bottle, and went to the reserve and got drunk. Sometimes I would end up at Talbert's father's house. His father and mother had split up. His father liked me. Thus the Restigouche Reservation became my second home. Little did I know at that time why I felt so at home on the reservation. In more recent years I have researched my true family's history and discovered I am a descendant from the Acadians of the 1600-1700's. I am Metis. In earlier days we were called half breeds. Acadians are a mixed people from the Wabanaki Confederacy consisting of the Eastern Tribes of Mi'kmaw (Mic Mac), Maliseet, Penobscot, Passamadquoddy and Abenaki.

At sixteen years of age, in 1968, my criminal record began. In jail I was introduced to marijuana. After my release I continued smoking pot and hash, and then progressed to pills and the rest of that stuff. One of the girls from my adopted family died of an overdose of drugs at thirty-nine years of age in 1992. Some die younger, some older! Death comes to all ages when you play with drugs. Sometimes it is intentionally, but other times it is just a mistake. When you cross the line in any addiction you get hooked. I had crossed the line in the mental realm of being a loser. I had crossed the line, and had become an alcoholic. Now I crossed the line and became a drug abuser.

As I look back now I realize I was fighting with the "real me" inside of me. I had an empty soul. I belonged to no one and had no place to really call home. I always believed there was a God, and presumed there was a devil. I didn't have a plan or purpose, and didn't care who lived or died. Life had treated me wrong. God saw my inner emptiness, and was beginning to answer one of my questions, even before I called out to Him. He knew I didn't know how to call on Him.

It happened like this. I was nineteen. We would go to people's houses to drink. We would drink and talk. In a small community like Campbellton with a population of 8000-10,000 it was easy to spot a newcomer. At Omer's house, this stranger was playing the harmonica. They told me that his name was Norman. He was older, maybe forty years old. He was a fun kind of guy, so we soon became drinking buddies. I would go over to his place sometimes, and then other times he would come to my adopted home and pick me up and we'd go drinking. After a few months, he went his way, and I went mine.

The following year I was drinking at a local bar, and had a few words with a man I thought was my real father. I said a few things that I shouldn't have said. I challenged him about how he had kept the other five boys, but had me disappear. Johnny wanted me to come to his house to get things straightened out. I refused that night since I didn't want to get into a fight. Later I met him, again, and went down to his house. Finally, I met my real mother. She had reconciled with her first husband. He knew about me, and wanted me to meet my mother. How was I supposed to know this! My mother then told me that my father was Norman Doucette. I laughed. This was hard for me to believe, since Norman was a tall man, 6' 2", and I was only 5' 2." Irene, looked at me, and insisted that that she was my mother and Norman was my father. She should know. Norman was gone, so I couldn't talk to him.

Summer 1977, I went into the bar, and there was Norman. He was kind of glad to see me. As I was talking, I asked him if he ever went out with a girl named Irene, from Richardville.

He got serious looking and said, "Yes."
"You had a child with her?" I continued.
He responded in a serious tone, "Yes."
I questioned him, "Was this child a boy or a girl?"
He responded, "Strike three, it was a boy!"
Then I declared, "You are looking at that boy right now!"

He had tears in his eyes. I told him that it was okay, at least we both knew the truth. I didn't see him during my years of incarceration. We did plan a visit in the summer of 1991 but this did not happen. He died in Ontario in 1992.

I thought now that I had found my true parents and had some identity that things were going to be different. Still there was an emptiness inside me. I couldn't understand this. I knew I was on the 'wrong train,' heading the wrong direction, but it kept moving, and so I traveled for another twenty years in this wilderness of drunkenness, crime, and prison, starting in 1968 until 1990. I just kept coming back to prison. I was never the model inmate. I was always is some kind of mess. I did my fair share of time in segregation. I was unlawfully at large, I believe, seven times from different institutions. While in prison, or in most of the 'joints', I worked in the kitchen. The reason being was that your food was better if you were working in the kitchen.

When I got released I would get drunk, and the fighting and stealing followed, and soon I was rewarded with another prison sentence. I couldn't trust myself anymore. I didn't know what I was capable of doing when drinking. Sin has its way of getting even, too. I was tired of this lifestyle, but didn't know how to get off this life's train going in the wrong direction. I knew there was a hell since I understood how separation had wrecked my life. I knew if I went to hell it certainly wouldn't make me any tougher or cooler. I didn't want to go to hell, but I didn't know how to bypass it. During those times in prison I had time to think about this. I realized I had found out who I was, but I also wanted to know why I was here on this earth. I needed a purpose. I was drifting like a ship without a rudder. I didn't want to go into a box in the ground, without accomplish anything. I had a long list of friends who were dead from knife wounds, gun shots, drugs and alcohol. I wanted to know where I was going when life's train reached its final destination.

I had believed in an Almighty God from my limited knowledge gained as a child. It was easier for me to accept Him as Almighty rather than a God who was personally interested in me. No one had been interested in me or taken the time to listen to me or help answer my questions. This was about to change, too. God is a gentleman and had waited for me to turn my attention to Him. He knew about my inner cry and that I wanted to make connection with Him but didn't know how or where to look. In 1982 when I was in New Carlisle Jail, on the Gaspe Coast in Quebec Province, I found a book in French called Reussir (To Succeed" in English) by Michel Quoist. It was Volume 14 on Spirituality. As I read this book, it started me searching within myself, and started to answer some of my questions. It talked about a personal Jesus who cared for me. I didn't know any Christians, and

85

had so many questions. This book became a treasure to me as it gave me glimmers of hope that there could be a purpose for my life. In all my years of roaming I kept and protected that book, and still have it to this day.

As soon as I was released it would be back to drinking and drugs, and back to jail in Fredericton, New Brunswick, Quebec City, Quebec, and Edmundston, New Brunswick or to prison in Springhill, Nova Scotia or Westmoreland Farm Camp – outside the walls of Dorchester Penitentiary. In April 1986 I was placed on remand until June. Then I was sentenced to twenty-two months. After a few months I was allowed to go to work in the woods cutting pulp wood. I was able to pay rent for a small trailer and live there while I served my time. I knew I was watched closely, so stayed away from drugs and booze. My job was completed so I was transferred to St. Godfoie, Quebec, to a foster home for ex-inmates. This was a new government program. This foster home did not work out, so I was transferred to another foster home in Paspebiac, Quebec. I appeared to be doing well, and was left in charge over the New Year 1987. We partied, and that was the end of my stay in this new foster program. I was sent 300 miles to a half-way house in Riviere du Loup, Quebec. I obtained employment and did well for a couple of months, and so was given a weekend pass to Campbellton . I spent the weekend drinking and ended up getting charged for robbery at Crosspoint, Quebec. I was taken in New Carlisle and sentenced to three years. In route to Laval, I received an additional 30 days for being unlawfully at large from Riviere du Loop. After thirty days in Montreal Reception in Laval, I was shipped to Cowansville, Quebec.

I was shipped to Springhill through Reception at Dorchester in November 1987.

I started to work on plans for my release. This time I was going to St. Leonard's House in Windsor, Ontario – a new place and a new start. I left Springhill, Nova Scotia, but never made it to Ontario. I got off the train in Campbellton, my hometown. I watched the train depart from the tavern across the street, and disappeared onto the Listiguj Indian Reserve for the next three weeks. When I did come across the inter-provincial bridge into Campbellton, a taxi driver spotted me, and reported it. I hadn't been in the bar more than a half an hour when four Royal Canadian Mounted Police came in both the side and front doors. I went quietly. I arrived back 'home' at Dorchester Reception on June 8. I realized my life was going nowhere. My thoughts turned again to the decision I had postponed from back in 1982 when I learned that Jesus could be a personal Saviour – not just an Almighty God, from the <u>Reussir</u> book. I knew there would be a Bible in my cell at Dorchester. I decided I was going to continue my search for God. All my life Jesus had been patiently waiting for me to come to Him. It finally happened on June 25, 1988, the day after my thirty-sixth birthday, while I was in Dorchester Prison. We had lunch at 11 a.m. and around 11:30 am I got down on my knees in my cell in C-5. I prayed a simple prayer from my heart. I didn't know much about Christianity but I was anxious to find out. I said, "Lord, if you are real like I have heard, and if you are resurrected and alive, and you don't turn anybody away, come into my heart. Direct my life because I have made a mess of everything. I confess my life of sin, I am tired and lonely, and ask your forgiveness. I believe you died on the Cross for my sin, and God raised you up on the third day." I got up off my knees and lay down on my bunk thinking there was going to be some kind of supernatural manifestation. Nothing happened. Then a peace came over me that I cannot explain in words. I knew I was a new person or 'born again'. I sensed it, I felt clean hearted.

I asked for a transfer to the Atlantic Institution, a new maximum prison in Renous, New Brunswick. Instead, I was charged for refusing to return Springhill Institution. Although I was a new 'born again' Christian because of that prayer in my cell, I didn't know about letting God's Word change my way of thinking. I decided that if they send me to Springhill, I wouldn't allow them to keep me in there!

God answered my prayers. On July 7, 1988 they came and told me the charges were dropped and I was transferred to Renous. Chaplain Gary Porter really encouraged me in my faith when I first arrived at the Atlantic Institution, in Renous. He helped me start the process of changing my name to its true identity. Monty Lewis, founder of Cons for Christ, brought in books from International Prison Ministry. These books told stories of how God had changed many ex-cons. I also read Monty's book Caper and Ernie's book Hooked that told of Canadian ex-inmates whose lives had been changed by Jesus. I figured if God could do this for them, and give them power to stay out of prison, then He could do the same for me.

When Gary Porter left this prison to take a church in Miramichi, Chaplain John Steward came into my life. He helped me to understand about Jesus, and how He died, and took my penalty for sin. He explained that Jesus came back alive after being in the grave three days. How because He is alive, He can give us power to say "No" to sin, and those things that come to destroy our lives. This was all new to me, but it felt so right inside of me. This was true love, someone loving me enough to give His life for me. I had never experienced such love. Jesus took the penalty – my sentence – for all the sins I had committed. He was condemned that I might go free. I realized that Jesus had died in my place, just like He had died in the place of Barabbas, the convict, who was set free during Jesus' trial in Jerusalem. Yes, I understood about 'sentencing' having been around the prison system for twenty years. My sins had sentenced me to death, but the gift of God, Jesus Christ, had made a way that I could by-pass hell. I could get off life's train that kept moving me closer to destruction. All it took was that simple prayer back in C-5, I understood it better now. John was a preacher of the Word,

The Bible, and the Truth of the Word, Jesus, was setting me free. I was amazed at how my life was changing. Then I met Captain Goodrich of the Salvation Army who helped me get involved in Bible Correspondence Courses. I was in prison but I felt like I was in heaven. The Holy Spirit was giving me spiritual food daily.

My second question was being answered, too. There was a purpose for my life. Life was now worth living. I was no longer alone. I belonged to the best family in the world, the family of God. God was my Father, and Jesus was my brother. I was a joint heir with Jesus, like it said in Romans 8:17.

I believed I was ready to leave prison on my mandatory supervision date. On December 29, 1988, I was given $50. and put on a plane in Chatham, New Brunswick. My destination was Orangeville, Ontario. The authorities believed a new location was the answer. I arrived in Orangeville on Friday night with two or three boxes of my life's personal effects. I had no place to go. Everything was locked up until Monday. My parole officer lived in Guelph, fifty miles away. I went to the police station with all my life's personal effects. I put them on the counter and told the cops that was where I was leaving them. They told me I couldn't leave my stuff there. I told them that I had to do this because I didn't have a place to go. I took the $50 and went to the tavern.

Now, I had just recently become a Christian in prison, but God will not force himself on anyone. I chose to walk into that bar. I started a conversation with Eddie, the cab's driver. He allowed me to stay with him at his mother's place till Monday. I met another man at that bar in Orangeville from Chatham, New Brunswick. He was a bricklayer, Gary Breau. He hired me. I drank after work each day. Twenty three days after arriving I decided to head back to New Brunswick. I was now unlawfully at large, since I hadn't said goodbye to my parole officer. I headed back to Restigouche Reserve. I was hiding from the law on the reserve for three weeks. I couldn't hide from God. We will reap what we sow. I had experienced this incredible unconditional love of God, but I had made a wrong choice to go to the tavern. I would have to pay for my violation of man and God's laws.

I was kept in Reception at Dorchester while they debated as to what to do with me.

I had not committed any crimes, but had left Ontario without advising my Parole Officer.

On March 16, 1989 they released me. I took the bus back home to Campbellton. The bus stopped, and I purchased some hard liquor and got back on the bus without drawing any attention to myself. When the bus arrived in my hometown, the bus driver had to call the police to take me off the bus. I was so drunk I couldn't identify myself. I crossed the bridge into Quebec Province, and did a robbery while drunk and on valium. The Quebec authorities transferred me back to be sentenced for my violations of parole. Here it was April, 1989, and I was heading back inside at the Atlantic Institution.

What had happened? I had made my decision to give my life to Jesus on June 25, 1988.

I was so happy. God had taken me to Renous and given me wonderful people who helped me.

I had been released December 29, 1988. I hadn't forgotten about my God. I had put Him in the back seat. Our Creator doesn't belong in the back seat. He needs to be Lord of All, or He is not Lord at all!

When I got back to my cell, I came clean with God. He didn't give up on me. He forgave me. We had to start all over again. This time I was determined to get stronger so I would not make this mistake again. I got back into my Bible Studies. I found that I should not depend on my own strength, but on Jesus Christ's. I could do all things through Christ that would strengthen me. It was not me, but Christ in me, that made the difference. Greater was Jesus, within me, than any temptation that would come my way. I had been told so many lies all my life, that to know Jesus couldn't and wouldn't lie to me was so liberating.

Chaplain Randy Fox, the new chaplain at Renous Prison continued to instruct me in my new life in Christ. It was in 1990 that Rev. Fox was instrumental in me obtaining my change of name. We did it through Fredericton, the province's capital. I changed my name to Peter Joseph Doucette, my biological father's last name. It had to be published in the newspaper for three weeks. Finally my name change was granted. The authorities in Renous Prison never said anything. After I was released I found out that this should not have taken place while I was in a federal prison. The moment that my name changed legally I could have walked out of prison, because there was no Peter Doucette who had been sentenced to serve 'time'. Well, there is always a first time for these things, and we learn something from each experience. I was thankful to Rev. Fox for his assistance – finally I was a new person in Christ, with my new correct name, with a new life ahead of me.

I was released on March 22, 1990. The prison guards told me in the hallways of Renous on the day of my release, that I would always be welcome back there. The life of a prison guard must be frustrating – seeing the same people returning again and again. In God's strength, I didn't plan to return. I moved to Bathurst, and rented a room on the second floor of the Gloucester Hotel on Main Street. This hotel also had a bar, and was a hotspot on weekends. The parole officer was telling me that the prison officials had wagers that I would be back in two or three weeks. Well, I didn't stay on the second floor very long, I moved to the third floor, because the noise from the bar was too much. I attended the life skills course during the day, and drove taxi at night. I attended AA meetings, and read my Bible and devotional book each day. God gave me the power and I didn't drink alcohol again. Alcohol was my drug of choice. I did battle with smoking dope, but I kept getting stronger, as I was getting to know more about Jesus. Just being around people who loved Jesus was a tremendous help.

On September 1990 I moved to Tracadie, New Brunswick, to follow up on a Tractor Trailer Course. I didn't do very well on the first course, so they gave me the opportunity to come back and do a second course. I didn't have much experience at driving a car, let alone a tractor trailer. When I did the course the second time, I didn't pass as far as the school was concerned, but I did get my license when tested. The driving school officials told me that I didn't have it in me and would never be a trucker. I had been told many times in my life that I wouldn't succeed. I was a new person now, and would not believe their words. With God I would succeed. I might not have the skill today, but I would have it, because I wasn't going to give up. I have been driving tractor trailer ever since across Canada, and to all forty-seven states of the United States of America.

While I was attending this Tractor Trailer Driving Course, we were billeted at various locations. Sometimes a group of us from the course would go out for coffee. I took particular notice of Therese, and made a point of speaking to her. We felt very comfortable talking to each other. She was a single mother. Her life was very different to mine. She was raised near Boston, in the Eastern United States. The first ten years of her education was in parochial schools, taught by nuns. She had married when she was twenty years old, and lost her husband in a car accident. She was expecting her second son, at the time of the accident. The next twenty years she spent raising her sons, and was employed at a Moncton Dairy as a delivery truck driver. She wasn't looking for a relationship when we met, but she gave me the impression that she did believe in giving someone a chance even if they had passed through difficult times. She had just come to upgrade her license, and after the eight week course, Therese, went back to her work in Moncton. We kept in touch and would visit on the weekends.

I decided to get baptized in water, just like Jesus did in the Jordan River. It was my public declaration of what Jesus had done in my life. Pastor of Christ Church in Moncton baptized me on December 2, 1991. As I went under the water in baptism I finally laid down the last of my old life, and came out of that water to walk in newness of life, and have never taken drugs again. Two months later I received the baptism of the Holy Spirit which has given me additional power to live this new life in Christ.

I know today without any doubt that it was Jesus, my Lord and Saviour, who took away the desire I had to drink and do dope. He took it to the Cross with Him. I could not stop on my own. I had proved this to myself too many times. I had messed up too many times. It is unthinkable that I take any credit for the good that has come into my life. No one, not my wife, not my parents, not a friend, not the government with all its programs, not any religion can take credit for the change that has taken and is taking place in my life daily. All credit is due to Jesus Christ, the Messiah! No one can know the profound misery of a convict but Jesus Christ. No one can really understand the emptiness inside a person's heart but Our Creator, the Lord Jesus.

On October 12, 1992, Therese and I were married and we have continued to live in Moncton.

As I look back on those early years, I realize how difficult it must have been for Therese to live with me. She, by the grace of God stayed with me, and helped me to understand myself. She has helped me in so many ways. We came from different backgrounds but we share the same faith in our Lord Jesus Christ. God has given me the opportunity to build a home, establish good credit, and start a business. Those things that I once thought impossible have become a reality, because of Him.

Our Home and Tractor Trailer

On November 21, 1996, I received my Official Pardon from the Government of Canada.

It was really special for me when I noticed that the Chairman of the National Parole Board that signed my Pardon Document was Willie Gibbs. He was the Warden of Springhill Institution when I served my sentence there in 1979. Even better still, is the fact that I am justified in the sight of God. Now 'justification' is one of those big theological words, but it can be explained completely in this little phrase, 'just as if I had never sinned'. Because of Jesus' sacrifice, I stand and will stand before Father God, just as if I had never sinned. There is no record of my crimes now or in eternity. Thank you, Jesus, for your gift of Salvation. It cost You everything, that I might have everything!

I am still driving tractor trailer today in 2006. He has been my Protector on the highways these last fifteen

Peter and Rose Doucette – 2005

years. There have been accidents, but He has kept me safe. I want to be the best trucker for Jesus. This might mean speaking to that driver at the next truck stop. No matter how small or large the task I want to be ready to give an answer to those who ask. I am *authentic* – I am the *real thing*. Jesus power has set me free and keeps me free from those addictions. I might work for a trucking company down here, but when all is said and done, I will finally answer to Him, at the end of my life's journey.

If God could take a nobody like me, without family or home, who became addicted to alcohol and dope, and make me a new person in Christ, then there is hope for you.

God *dealt* with me so personally. He answered my questions.

Who am I? I have found my true identity in Jesus, and God's family. As a bonus he also helped me find my father and mother, and has allowed me to trace my ancestry back to 1700's.

Why am I here? Jesus has given me a purpose in life. I am able to let my life speak for Christ. I am the only 'Bible' that some people will read. I pray by my walk and my talk to direct others to Jesus.

Where am I going? I know where I am going when I get to the end of life's journey. I have everlasting life, John 3:16. I have a home (sure beats a prison cell) down here on earth, but Jesus has prepared a mansion, for me in the future. John 14:2-3. The best thing is that I will never be separated from Father God.

Check out the prayer and the pages at the back of this book or call out to Him from your inner being. Get to know Jesus through His Word, the Bible. Find a home church where you can keep growing in Jesus. Jesus will *deal* with your deep hurts and addictions and *deliver* you. He will restore those wasted years. You will be amazed at what Jesus will do!

Peter Doucette
c/o Truth Tabernacle of Greater Moncton
50 Lonsdale Drive
Moncton, N.B.
E1G 2G3

Chapter Four

TROUBLED TEEN'S TURNABOUT

The Life
of
Troy Mcleod

Troubled Teen's Turnabout

I was born in Newaashiiniigmiing, which means land surrounded by water in the Ojibwa language. The name given to this place in English is Cape Croker. It is on the Bruce Peninsula, in Western Ontario. This peninsula points like a finger into Georgian Bay of Lake Superior which is one of the Five Great Lakes of Canada. This First Nations Reservation is a beautiful place surrounded by trees, water and bluffs. Whenever I am up that way, I am amazed at God's creation. I did not remember this beauty as a child since my family left this wonderful country for the city of Kitchener-Waterloo, Ontario, when I was only five years old.

The reason we left the reservation was my parents separated, and later divorced. I do not know all the details of their separation, but I do know that my father's drinking was a contributing factor. I have often wondered what it would have been like if my parents had not separated. Maybe my mother did it out of protection for us children? We cannot change the past, but I must admit that this made me very sad at times, and other times it has made me very angry. I was sad that my siblings and I missed out on having a father to discipline, encourage, and provide us with the love that we needed. I was angry at my mom and dad because they didn't stay together and work out their differences and give the best they could for their children.

I was the youngest of the children when my mother moved to the twin cities of Kitchener-Waterloo, Ontario. I was five years old and my older sister, Jenine, was seven years old. I have two older brothers, Trevor and Donnie, who were nine and eleven years old at the time. Needless to say, I felt the benefits of being the youngest until my younger sister Jilane was born. My mother was pregnant with Jilane when we moved into the city. Of all my siblings, Jenine and I became the closest, due to our age and common interests.

Troy McLeod - Lacrosse League - 1988

I remember helping her with her newspaper route. Later as teenagers, we worked at the same restaurant.

From an early age, I looked up to my brothers. I believe because my father was absent, I was looking for a male role model. My brothers were older than me, and they didn't want their little brother tagging along with them. On numerous occasions, my brothers told me to scram and go back home. I felt more rejected by my brothers than I did by anybody in my family, and this included my father. Their rejection was more personal and continued through the years. I did not blame my brothers for this rejection because they were dealing with their own struggles of growing up

99

by themselves. I tried to be more like my brother, Trevor, because I looked more like him. In my teen years, I started to walk in the footsteps of my older brothers trying to be the tough guy.

Being the tough guy was never in my nature. The following event from my early childhood illustrated this fact. This involved my friend Jake. It happened the day we moved to Kitchener-Waterloo from the Reservation. I was helping to unload the boxes from the van and carrying them into our new house. Jake purposely blocked my path. He tried to push me. I felt scared, not tough, but pretended nothing happened. Sometime later, Jake and I became best friends. We were both five years old. He was the typical blonde-haired white kid, and I was the typical dark-haired tanned kid. We had a lot of fun hanging out together. Jake proved to me that he was not the tough guy when we went tree climbing. We had this special big tree behind our townhouse we loved to climb. One time, Jake climbed too high into the tree and when he looked down, he got scared and screamed for help. Firemen had to come and rescue him.

When I was six years old, we moved to another part of the city. I hoped to see him again, but Jake died at the age of nine in a townhouse fire with his Grandpa and his two sisters.

I biked halfway across the city and saw the charred ruins of their house, my heart ached and I cried. From this point on, life and death became a reality.

I was able to make friends easily at my new school. Most of my teachers were friendly, and treated me like any other student. I would love it when my teachers would tell stories about their lives. Mr. Auld, my grade four teacher, told the most humorous stories. I remember in mathematics class, Mr. Auld held competitions for the students. I would often be the winner, or be in second place. There were other times when I found school an academic challenge. I believe in these subjects, homework was required. Homework was not encouraged at home. Actually, I liked this as it gave me more time to hang around with my friends after school. We'd have fun exploring construction sites of new apartment buildings and new homes that were being built in the city. Some of these construction sites were on the outskirts of the city and near the Grand River. As a result we would swim up and down the river all afternoon. As I think back now, I realize it was very dangerous, but my friends and I had no one to tell us of this danger.

In grade six, I started to notice that all my friends came from my neighbourhood. They all came from government housing townhouses, just like me. I also noticed that most of them came from single parent homes, just like me. This difference became a reality when I would be invited to a friend's house from another neighbourhood. I noticed they lived in two car garage houses, and both dad and mom were home.

When I wasn't hanging out with friends, I was playing sports. I was involved in city house league sports like hockey, football and lacrosse. These sports experiences were some of the best memories I have as a child. It was a way to win approval from my father. It meant a lot to me to have my father watch my sports games. Sometimes, my older brother and I would go on the city bus with my hockey equipment to these games. I even remember my brother coming into my dressing room and tying my laces for me. At the time, it meant a lot to me, because many of the boys in my dressing room had their fathers there lacing them up.

When I was older, I remember meeting one of the guys from my hockey team at a party, and we started talking about the times we used to play hockey. Since doing drugs at this time was the "cool thing," he thought I would enjoy his story. He told me that before one of our games, he remembered going outside and seeing my brother "smoking up" before he came into the dressing room to help me with my skates. I could not blame my old teammate for trying to be cool, but I instantly felt like one of my best memories with my older brother was suddenly false and no longer worth recalling.

I vividly remember one year when we were in the middle of a hockey tournament, around Christmas time, I had a court appearance for some theft charges. I was so anxious about getting out after my court appearance in time for the next game that I kept turning around and looking at the clock at the back of the courtroom. I was hoping it would be finished on time so I could play in the tournament. Unfortunately, the judge interpreted my turning around as sign of not caring about the situation, and therefore, thought that two weeks in open custody over Christmas would serve me well. I remember being so crushed. I was just a kid and there is no way I could fully comprehend the implications of my actions on others and my teammates at the time. In fact, this two week detention started me on a whole new road; a new direction which I traveled down for the next few years.

About this time, between grades six and seven, I started to make wrong choices. My wrong choices started when I chose to hang around certain people. We were not good influences on each other. We started to skip school and create mischief. This mischief usually meant stealing from the convenience store or the department stores in the malls. At this time, the cigarettes were sold on the front counter in display racks. Nobody wanted these new brands. My friends and I didn't mind the brand of cigarette, as we smoked them and didn't pay for them. I had no idea how addictive cigarettes would become in my life. Occasionally, the police would catch us wandering around late at night, and take us home for the evening. When morning came, I would be out the house, and disappear for a couple more days.

On one of these occasions, the police picked us up and charged us with theft. Since I was a young offender, I was put in open custody at a place called Anchor House in Kitchener.

This was a division of Ray of Hope Ministries run by Christian Mennonites. Over the next two weeks while in detention there, I started to read the Picture Bible. I was just amazed at what the Bible was saying. It reminded me of the times when I was a small boy and had gone to Sunday school and heard similar stories. When I was released, I went home. A guy named Steve, a staff member from Anchor House, came to visit me. He brought me my own brand new Picture Bible. This act of kindness really touched my heart. Just to think he cared enough about me to give me such a great gift meant so much to me.

My family moved again to a new part of the city. My life did not change. It seemed to improve for about two years. This was because I had to find a part-time job in order to pay restitution for my crimes. This was an Order from the Judge. It was a good order and did help me for a short time. It didn't take me too long to meet and make friends in my new neighbourhood. These friends were just like my old friends.

I was now in grade nine. My brothers were already involved in drugs, and one of them set me up with one of his friends to sell drugs at school. I thought it was the coolest thing being in grade nine and having grade eleven and twelve students coming to me for LSD, mushrooms or hash. I enjoyed the popularity, but soon realized when you have drugs, everybody is your friend. I was working at a restaurant as a bus boy and soon I was selling drugs to my coworkers. It was at this time that Serge Le Clerc, whose story is also in this book, came to our school. Serge spoke in the Assembly Hall to all the students. I remembered meeting Serge because he volunteered at the Anchor Open Custody Facility where I had been held in custody when I was younger. Serge told about his life of crime and drugs, and how he had spent twenty one years in prison because of his drug abuse. He told how his life had been changed. I believe it was a warning to all the students. I didn't want to listen as I had already started to use drugs. Soon, I was using more drugs than I was selling.

Once I started using drugs, things went downhill fast. I quit my job, and dropped out of school in grade nine.

I was hanging out with other teen drug addicts. Any money I was making from selling drugs was quickly spent on alcohol and partying. Eventually the money started to run out, and I was therefore, forced to pursue criminal activities in order to maintain my lifestyle. This meant break and entries into homes and businesses and fencing the stolen property to a couple of guys who lived in the neighbourhood. These guys were a lot older than me. They were in their mid to late twenties. I was fourteen years old. Due to the age difference, my friends and I feared them, thinking they were the toughest guys'. This fear meant stealing more stuff for them and receiving twisted admiration from them. I write "twisted" because I now realize that these older guys were not tough or real men. When you think about it, all these guys were doing was pushing around a bunch of fourteen year old teenagers from their neighbourhood. The friendship I thought I had with them was quickly dashed to pieces one night. My buddy and I pulled off a score that gave us $2000 in cash and some stolen merchandise. Needless to say, we met with these guys to discuss the stolen merchandise and how we might get rid of it. My friend and I kept the cash we obtained a secret. Nobody could be trusted. Once we had spent most of the money, we decided to tell this guy about it. This was more for bragging rights than anything else. As soon as the words were out of our mouths, this guy reached across a table and grabbed my friend by the shirt and slapped him. He told us to take him home immediately. I was expecting a hand to come across the table and grab me. Fortunately, that did not happen. After that event, I was left with a sickening feeling.

Eventually, this criminal activity led me to the greener pastures of a smaller southern Ontario city called Stratford. I was caught stealing a car, arrested and held in custody. I was sent to Hope Manor, a closed custody facility also administered by Ray of Hope Ministries.

This place was in a small community called Petersburg, Ontario. While I was there, a group of us teenagers who were in custody decided to riot. The plan was to take out one of the guards and use his keys to unlock the doors and walk straight out of the building. We thought we had the numbers to overpower any staff working that night. As I look back now, I realize God knew our plans long before we did, and made sure there was a staff meeting being held in the building the same night that we decided to hold the riot. When the broken pieces of furniture started to fly across the room and shattered the glass in the windows, there was plenty of additional male staff to handle the situation. We could not understand how they appeared out of nowhere. After a brief standoff, we were all restrained and taken to our rooms. Out of the whole event, one thing that stuck with me and wedged itself in my heart were the expressions of the staff members' faces, especially a man named Conrad. All the young offenders in custody liked him because he treated us with respect, and we could sense the compassion he had in his heart for others. I remember being locked into my room and as I looked out the window, I saw Conrad staring at me with tears in his eyes. It just hit me how I must have made this man feel. All of us cursing, fighting and spitting on the staff. I believe this staff had a real concern for us, but we were determined to follow our own way. With the riot over I waited for my court date. The entire time we wondered whether we were going to be charged for this riot.

I went before the judge on my charge in Stratford, and he sentenced me to another eight months on top of the four months I was already serving. This totaled a one year closed custody sentence. In the court proceedings, my lawyer argued about the incorrect procedures the police officers used in my arrest. Due to this, he felt the charges should be dropped. The judge did not care and still sentenced me. Later, the charges were dropped, but I had completed the sentence. Privately, my lawyer mentioned the speech the judge gave during my sentencing. The judge mentioned issues surrounding aboriginal people. According to my lawyer, if I were non-native, I would have been spared the long speech and the long sentence. This was the first time I remember feeling different because I was Native or from the First Nations. Ironically, I didn't realize it until my lawyer pointed it out to me. Native or not, I still had to do my time. I returned to Hope Manor following my court date.

They decided that I needed to be transferred to a more secure facility. In the meantime, the Director continued to hold me at Hope Manor. As I have already mentioned, Hope Manor was Christian and so they offered chapel services as part of their program. Many of the young men used to go just to get out and see other people, in particular the younger women who would come to the services every now and then. On more than one occasion, we ended up creating a disturbance by laughing and joking. In spite of all this, I kept going to these meetings.

I started hearing things again that I had read about in my Picture Bible. I recall that at one meeting they told us that Jesus was someone who would never leave you. I had never had such a deep friendship. All my friendships had been shallow and based on selfish interest. Nobody truly cared for me. My relationship with my family was distant in this period of my life, and deep relationships were seemingly non-existent. As I was growing up, we were a family living under one roof, but everybody lived for themselves. As I got older, I lived for myself. I am sure my mother loved, provided and cared for us, but there was no deep connection between us. Now they said that Jesus loved me and died for me. This was hard for me to understand. Why? They said that it was because Jesus wanted to take my sentence or penalty for my sin so that I didn't have to go to hell. This made me think about my present life and life after death. I knew about death, and that it could come at any time. Jake, my friend, died when he was just nine years old. I was fearful about my destiny if I died. Eventually, I came to the point where I made a verbal commitment to become a Christian. I was willing to trust what these people said was true and I put my faith in Jesus. A group of people from the Prison Fellowship from Kitchener, Ontario, were taking the chapel the night that I prayed. I asked God to forgive me of my sins because His son, Jesus, had died in my place. I knew that God's Holy Spirit was in my life after I accepted Jesus as my Saviour. This was evident when I went back to my room and cracked open my Bible for the first time and understood the words in a meaningful way. I believe God kept me for those few weeks after my sentencing and while they were organizing my transfer, so that I could receive His Truth from the staff and all these volunteer groups that would come in to share in the chapel.

The facility they transferred me to was the St. John's Training School in Uxbridge just outside of Toronto. It was a much bigger place. There were about a hundred young offenders about my own age. The property of this facility was split into a north and south side. They had an outdoor swimming pool and an outdoor ice rink. It even contained a coveted welding shop. Everybody tried to go there. Why? You could smoke cigarettes and avoid detection by blowing the smoke up the arc metal exhaust pipes. The facility was surrounded by two-storey fences. There was no way I was going to escape this place. The only way a person could get out those doors was if his behavior enabled him to obtain a high enough level to receive a pass. This usually took a long time as the staff needed to recommend the individual. There were many young offenders, so how could they get to know us? St. John's Training School was easier for me to handle because of my recent decision to follow Jesus. I endeavoured to keep to the rules in order to get privileges. I remember thinking for the first time about how my actions affected others. Don't get me wrong, I didn't receive an instant halo.

I still had many struggles in my life and still treated others badly at times, but it was from this moment on that I knew that my new struggles were not going to be on my own.

When I finished my one year as a young offender at this closed custody, I was released.

I quickly gravitated towards and found the acceptance again with old friends who did alcohol and drugs. I had accepted Jesus as Saviour, but I chose to walk away and do my own thing. I depended on my own strength rather than God's strength.

Over the next three years as I abused alcohol and drugs, my life crumbled. I was in and out of adult jail a couple times. I became very withdrawn and depressed. Other times, I would become paranoid and be very volatile. Due to all this, I was taken a couple of times for assessment and spent some periods of time in the psychiatric ward. Since I had become a Christian and had experienced true peace then, I had no peace whatsoever in the lifestyle that I was living at this time. I knew I needed help.

I did attend church for a while when I was seventeen years old, but somehow, I could not live this Christian life. It was during this time that I sat through a church service and I heard some men from Teen Challenge give their testimonies about how God, through Jesus Christ, had changed their lives. I sat in the back pew, and thought that there is no way I was like these guys. I was blind and oblivious about my own lifestyle.

Later on in my life when I became desperate, I thought about that meeting and the guys from Teen Challenge, and made the phone call to apply for the Teen Challenge Farm in the London, Ontario. This was a voluntary one year program where you enrolled so that you could be set free from drugs and alcohol. I almost didn't make it to the London Teen Challenge because my brother and his girlfriend tried to discourage me. They thought that I didn't need the structure provided by Teen Challenge. I knew I needed this structure if I was going to make lasting changes in my life. I had tried on my own and could not break free. I knew I needed God's strength.

Teen Challenge really meant business. After all, Teen Challenge had been around since the late 1950's. It all started as a result of a young and caring pastor in Pennsylvania, Rev. David Wilkerson. He saw on television hurting youth in gangs in the ghettos of the city of New York. God challenged him to share His love with them and told him that He could change their lives. God transformed lives. These youth were living on the street so they needed a place to live. They needed a place where they could receive God's Word so they could stay free of drugs, alcohol and violence. Teen Challenge was born.

Today, Teen Challenge is in 82 countries, with 611 outreaches worldwide. The farthest southern outreach is in Perth, Australia, and the farthest northern outreach is Kultan, Siberia.

In Canada, there is a Teen Challenge Centre in Moncton, New Brunswick and in Lotbiniere, Quebec under the title "Defi Jeunesse Inc". In Ontario, there is the Teen Challenge Farm in London, and a Centre in Sault Ste. Marie in Northern Ontario. Another centre will be opened soon near Toronto. In Manitoba, the Teen Challenge Centre is in Winnipeg. The Saskatchewan Teen Challenge is just outside of Saskatoon. The Director there at this time is Serge LeClerc, whose story is in this book. This is the same Serge who I met when I was first in custody at Anchor House in Kitchener, and who came to speak at my High School. The Alberta Teen Challenge is in Calgary, and there is another Teen Challenge in Vancouver, British Columbia.

To be accepted into residence at Teen Challenge, I had to submit to medical tests to prove I was not on any drugs or medication. Since I had been on medication in the psychiatric ward, I went to my father's place for a couple of weeks to get off medication. Once the medications were out of my system, I was accepted into the Teen Challenge Program.

As we drove through the gates of Teen Challenge Farm, I sat back and surveyed the beautiful property, trying to ignore the nervousness in my stomach. I didn't know what to expect, but I knew in my heart that I needed to be there. I needed to experience again that peace that I had experienced for that short time when I was in Hope Manor. Mentally, I wasn't in the best frame of mind since I had just come from jail and the psychiatric hospital. It took me about two months to get my bearings because I didn't know who to trust. Here I was expected to live in close proximity to other men in a dormitory. They were patient with me, and showed me love and respect. In time, I learned that I could trust the staff members who worked at Teen Challenge. As we put into practice the principle we studied from God's Word, I started to experience positive changes in my life. Many great things happened in my life while at Teen Challenge. Not only did I experience freedom from a destructive lifestyle, but most importantly, I learned from the Bible what it meant to live a Christian life. Although I had made a commitment to follow Jesus before, I had never learned how to walk as a Christian. I did my own thing, in my own strength, and failed. I learned to depend on the Almighty's strength so I could handle any situation. This was the great turnabout in my life. As I said before, I had not been doing well mentally, but I believed God's Word and He healed me. He restored my sanity. It was not a certain staff member's teaching or wisdom, but God who changed my life, and He deserved all the praise. God certainly used the Teen Challenge Program to break the chains of sin in my life. I always enjoyed the weekly chapel services when we would have special speakers come and speak to us. I also enjoyed the many times of prayer. We were not just told to pray, but we were shown how to pray, and how to know the voice of God who would direct our lives.

I was thankful for the balanced program that Teen

Challenge offered. We were required to do our chores, and become responsible in our work areas. I had never experienced this balance of responsibilities in my life, and needed this practical instruction. We had the choice of working in the area of our interest. We could choose to work in the farming, kitchen, woodworking, or vehicle restoration area. I needed to learn about a work ethic if I was going to survive in life once I left the Teen Challenge Program.

Another aspect of Teen Challenge that I was grateful for was the friendships that I formed with other students. These friendships were not shallow like I had experienced with other drinking and drug buddies, but were deep with meaning and purpose because we knew we were all members of God's Family.

I learned to trust God to look after every one of my needs. For example, all the clothing I needed, God provided. Specifically, I remember this really nice fall black jacket I was given. Another student at the centre received it from his family. He didn't want it, so he said I could have it. I believe to this day that God provided this jacket for me. I wore that coat for six years, until the inside was so worn out that my future wife begged me to get rid of it. Needless to say, it was eventually replaced.

When I completed the one-year program at Teen Challenge we had a Graduation Ceremony. The ceremony was open to family and friends. My father attended my Graduation. This was a big deal for me. I had not graduated from high school, so this was my first graduation. This graduation was momentous for me because I had never completed anything in my life until then. I knew that in God's strength, anything was attainable! I have now gone through other graduation ceremonies since Teen Challenge, but none have meant the same because this graduation marked the turnabout in my life. The statistics still stand that 86% of graduates of the Teen Challenge Program worldwide remain drug-free after five years. I am pleased to be part of that percentage. Secular rehabilitation statistics range between 12-15%. Jesus makes the difference!

After the Teen Challenge program, I still felt the need to continue in my Christian education. I believed that I needed to be far away from the pulls of the old lifestyle for a longer period of time. I prayed about it and decided to attend a Bible College located in a small town in the province of Saskatchewan. The college was a Full Gospel Bible College. Once again, I learned more from God's Word during these three years of study. I learned to walk daily in close relationship with Jesus. At the time I intended to become a pastor, but as time went on, I did not feel this calling as strong in my life. This does not mean I will not be a pastor in the future. Our lives are in God's Hands.

In my first year, I was able to get involved in leadership at the Bible College as I was asked to be a Resident Assistant in one of the dormitories. I really felt honored to be asked to hold a leadership position in my first year in Bible College. I continued to be Resident Assistant in my second year. Then in my third year, I ran for Student Body President at the Bible College and was voted into this position by my peers. God was certainly changing this fearful and depressed person into a person with leadership qualities. The three years while I was at Bible College, I grew so much more both spiritually and emotionally. One of the greatest lessons I learned was that Jesus came from heaven to earth to restore us to a right relationship with His Heavenly Father. Jesus took the first step and reached out to us. Likewise, we need to take the first step to reach out to other people with God's love, even before they reach out to us for help.

During my last summer at Bible College, I was at a church picnic that was being held by the Saskatchewan River. The summer had just started and some of my friends and I thought it a good idea to go swimming in the river. One of the guys went down to the river ahead of us. As a group of us were making our way down to the river, we heard a strange

commotion coming from the river. I had taken first-aid training, so I ran down the river. When I got there I saw my friend
screaming for help. I yelled to him to relax and stay above
water. He was hysterical. There was no way he heard my
voice. He went under the water and didn't come back up, so I
jumped into the river and swam out to him. I was able to grab
him and started pulling him toward the shore. Some men in
a canoe came to my assistance. My friend was revived but
spent a few weeks in the hospital. The police officer on the
scene told me that there were many people who had drowned
in this river and commended me on my willingness to jump
in the water to save somebody. He nominated me for a Medal
of Bravery. I was flown to Ottawa and received the Medal of

Presentation of Medal of Bravery by Governor General
Adrienne Clarkson to Troy McLeod
in Ottawa - December 2000

113

Bravery from the then Governor General, Adrienne Clarkson, in the winter of 2000.

After completing my three years of Bible College in Eston, Saskatchewan, I worked with the Ministry of Teen Challenge in Sault Ste. Marie, Ontario, for two years. While I was in Sault Ste. Marie, I met my wife Katie. She was in Sault Ste. Marie at the time taking an aviation course at the local college. We were married the next year in 2002. I thank God for giving me a wonderful wife, who loves Jesus, and we want to work together to reach out to others with the love of Jesus.

I had given some thought to a career in medicine. We prayed about it, and Katie and I both felt that combining a career in medicine with her aviation training would be useful in working for the Lord in the future. Due to the fact that I had dropped out of high school in grade nine, I didn't have the necessary academic requirements to succeed in university. It seemed like a goal that I could not attain. I have applied myself over the years and it has not always been easy. With God's help and the encouragement and support of my wife, I am now in my last year of my Microbiology Degree at the University of Saskatchewan. I recently finished writing the Medical College admissions test and I will apply to medical schools this fall. With God, all things are possible!

God has turned my life around since I made that right choice at Hope Manor and followed it through when I entered the Teen Challenge Program. Since then, God has directed me each step of the way. He has restored relationships within my family. I know in my early years, I did not represent my family well and caused them grief and pain. I'm so thankful that I can now talk openly to both of my parents, and to the rest of my family members without guilt or shame.

Even more amazing is that I am continually offered the grace and the forgiveness for my sins when I make a wrong choice in life. None of us are perfect, and daily, we

Mr. & Mrs. Troy and Katie McLeod - May 10, 2002

need the Lord's cleansing. 1 John 1: 9 says "If we confess our sins, He is faithful and just to forgive us our sins, and cleanse us from all unrighteousness." This verse was written to Christians. We need to clean the windshields of our minds and hearts daily through His Word so we can see and do what God has for us.

I am thankful that I made that right choice to seek Jesus when I was young so now I have many years that I can put to use to bring others to Him. My heart goes out to teenagers and youth who are addicted and struggling with the chains of drugs, alcohol and others sins that have made them prisoners. I was there, but Jesus set me free, and He can do the same thing for you.

Call out to Him. He loves you. He will forgive you. He will free you from your habits. He will give you His power to live for Him. Be sure to keep in God's Word and in fellowship with other Christians so you will be encouraged to walk in His Ways. Your future is with God is Great! (Jeremiah 29:11)

Troy McLeod
c/o Teen Challenge Farm
P.O. Box 777
London, Ontario
N6P 1R6

Chapter Five

BACK FROM THE BELLY OF THE BEAST

The Life Story
of
Serge LeClerc

Back From The Belly Of The Beast

I am a product of rape. My mother, a young girl of mixed race – white and red, gave birth to me in an abandoned building. My teenaged mother decided to migrate to Toronto. At that time in the late 1940's, Toronto was supposed to be paved with gold. It did not matter where people came from. They could go there and make a new beginning. Unfortunately, she could only speak Cree and French while Toronto was an English city and this made things quite difficult for her. Not only was she unable to speak the language, she was also unable to read and write it. She settled into an area within the inner city nicknamed 'Cabbage Town' which surrounded the concrete jungle of the Regent Park Projects. My first eight years were spent there, and they were amongst the happiest years of my life. We all had the common enemy of poverty; therefore, it did not matter what colour we were, what culture we belonged to, or where we came from. As we looked to feed and clothe ourselves, we were all equal.

I lived in a Chinese rooming house for those first eight years of my life. My mother told me that before I was five years old, I could speak French, Cree, and Chinese, but I couldn't speak English. I was considered quite lucky in my neighbourhood because my mother never beat or hit me. My mother worked two jobs, a day job and a night job, as a dishwasher. I was considered even luckier that I didn't have a father, as strange as that sounds, because many of my friends had fathers who were alcoholics who often took the welfare cheque or whatever money was in the house. This often left the households without food. Not only did I have food and care but often my mother and I would take any extra food that we had to the poorer families in the 'hood.'

When I was eight-years-old, I played hooky from school on a spring day with a group of other boys. We went shoplifting uptown on a Friday afternoon and I had short legs. In the early 1950's, under the Juvenile Delinquency

Act, a truant was charged under the Status Offence section of the Act. According to the social philosophy of the time, if a child lived with a single mother and he was a boy child, and then he got into trouble, it was because he was improperly parented. Obviously they thought that single mothers lacked the ability to deal with boys and, of course, since my mother could not read and write, she was placed in another category altogether. At eight years of age, I was taken to 311 Jarvis Street for the weekend. It was the central holding facility for juvenile offenders while going to court and before sentencing. Upon entering the courtroom, I saw my mother sitting across the room with men in black flowing gowns sitting behind desks and another behind a high pedestal looking down upon everyone like a big crow on a tree top. I was sentenced to St. John's Training School as a delinquent, but what I remember the most was their calling my mother an unfit mother. Going to St. John's Training School with those words echoing in my mind, I was angry with my mother. I was angry because she didn't tell them that she was not an unfit mother, and I was angry with my mother for letting them take me away.

St. John's Training School, run by an order of Christian Brothers, in the history of Canada, has become synonymous with violence, brutality, sexual abuse, rape, and crippling beatings. As an eight year old boy I was very quickly earmarked for special treatment as a result of being part Indian, a product of rape, and a bastard. I found myself in an environment that was permeated with a regime of violence. Discipline at St. John's was immediate and harsh. For instance, when I was nine year old, my jaw was broken for speaking in chapel. The Christian Brother just hauled off and punched me to quiet me down. Whatever feelings I had towards his God were cemented that day when a six-foot, two-hundred-pound man knocked me out cold and broke my jaw for speaking during chapel. I very quickly rebelled. I became a runaway or, what is called in prison language, a go-boy.

Just by the nature of being brought up in the inner city, I had developed a different way of thinking about life, managing life, and being a little bit more in control. Everyday, we dealt with drunks in the gutter, drug addicts with needles in their arms, poverty, and our friends eating ketchup sandwiches because their fathers were on a drunken binge. Therefore, it was not beyond expectation for me to run. Of course, I ran to Toronto, right back to the same old neighbourhood where I was immediately arrested and brought back to the training school. They punished me each and every time, but I would await my chance to go-boy again and again. Of course, it became more difficult for the police to find me as time went on as I discovered other areas of the city in which to hide.

Every time I was brought back, I was first taken to solitary confinement. Eight rooms, I believe, were used for solitary confinement, rooms no bigger than a clothes closet. I had to curl around the corners of the confined space, with no lights, no windows, and no toilet. Rather, there was a plastic bucket. The door was solid, made of hardwood slats, without a window. Kept in the nude, I was put in there from three to seven days. This was to correct me, but, of course, all it did was make me angrier. I ran away more often. I ran to abandoned buildings and heated garages. I stole food out of gardens, dairy trucks, and bakeries, and ate out of garbage bins in the back of restaurants and grocery stores.

There was a staff member at this place who had an infamous form of punishment for me because I had become a bit of a thorn in his side. As he was the man who was directly in charge of me, every time I escaped, he was the one who got the brunt of the Administration's wrath for not being able to manage this young boy.

I was not the only boy he abused of course, but to me, it seemed that I received it more than anyone else during my stay there. He would begin by stripping me nude in front of the other boys in the barracks. There was nothing more humiliating to a child, especially a boy who was underdeveloped, than to be stripped nude in front of peers and not be able to cover his private parts. I was made to hold two small buckets of sand at arm's length straight out from my sides. He stood behind me with a sawed-off goalie stick. The sawed-off goalie stick was minus the blade so that all he had was the centrepiece in which he had drilled holes.

Eventually when my arms would droop past a certain level that he chose over a time span (of course, he was the only one with a watch), I would hear the whistle of the hockey stick as it went through the air behind me and brace myself as he hit me across the buttocks and the back of the legs. This would knock me down on my knees. I would immediately get back up again. The drilled holes acted like little suction cups that would cause blood blisters across my back and buttocks.

I still carry the scars from those blood blisters, however, the biggest scars came from his mouth. He called me squaw, garbage, loser, bastard, and many other vile names. Every time this fine representative of God scarred me with his mouth, it went into my soul. If a child is called "bad" long enough, then he becomes bad. It is a self-fulfilling prophecy. The more he called me bad, the more I acted out.

At the age of ten, after spending two years at St. John's Training School, I hit the front page of the newspapers for what was to be the first of many times. Authorities caught me selling cigarettes on a street corner after stealing a station wagon filled with cartons of cigarettes. The newspapers made a big thing out of a ten year old hot-wiring and stealing a car, while living underneath a porch of an empty mansion on one of the most prestigious streets in Toronto. This immediately hit the front page of the Toronto Telegram. This was also a big embarrassment for the St. John's Training School because once again, I had escaped.

I knew that when I arrived back in St. John's, I was going to face that man once again with his ugly form of punishment. My plan was to go to the stable as soon as I got out of the paddy wagon and break off a pitchfork prong to use as a weapon. I walked into that sawed-off-goalie-stick-beating man's office and buried about six inches of that prong into his belly. When they took me to 311 Jarvis Street and court, they said that I had to be brain-damaged. For a boy to be so violent in attacking a full-grown man, he must be brain-damaged.

A new process then began. I had developed an attitude that many people develop when they are either messing up their lives, making wrong choices, getting involved with drugs or alcohol, or suffering a lot of pain. It is the "I don't care" attitude. Often in response to the questions "What are you doing?" or "How do you feel?" the answer is: "I don't care. It doesn't bother me." This response becomes protective armour. We try to pretend that nothing bothers us. We don't care. At the tender age of ten, I had already become an expert at it. It is something that we do to protect our insides from the pain that goes on in our lives, the wrong choices that we make, and the burdens that we carry.

At ten years old, when I walked into court that day, I had already become an expert at "I don't care." I had the swagger of Cabbage Town. The Judge said, "I'm sending you to a maximum security place. You are brain-damaged." I said, "I don't care." As I walked out of the courtroom, I said, "Brain-damaged, that's kind of cool. Brain-damaged! Gee, I betcha there aren't too many people they say that about." I began to wear that as a label of which to be proud.

They then sent me to a place called the Ontario Training School, a maximum security facility for much older boys, hooked onto Guelph Reformatory. A guard made the point the day I arrived that he was there to instruct me, and since I had such a record of being a Go-Boy, he could assure me that this place was escape-proof and that at ten years old, I would not get the best of him.

Two years later, I escaped again the third time, by

setting the gymnasium on fire to distract the staff while stealing a truck to crash it through the gate in the fence. Later, I had to give myself up to the Ontario Provincial Police on the Trans-Canada Highway after I drove the truck into a gully. They took me back to court at twelve years old and said that I was irreparably brain-damaged.

They said that they couldn't control my behaviour or my violent tendencies. They decided that they were placing me in a group home. That was the biggest insult anybody had ever given to me. There was never any thought of returning me to my mother. To them my mother was an unfit parent, so they put me in the care of the government. They decided to put me into a group home while making it a point to tell me that this group home dealt with children that no one else wished to deal with. That one short sentence inflicted the greatest amount of pain that I experienced in those four years. Putting me in a place with children that no one else wanted to deal with indicated to me that I was one of those children: unwanted, impossible to deal with, undesirable and unworthy. Of course, I immediately ran away that night. I jumped out of a second floor window from a bathroom, wearing only a pair of jockey shorts! I would take the world on – on my terms.

Three short years later, I was a gang leader. In an era when guns were almost unheard of, I was carrying a handgun. I'm not a very big man, but what I needed to make up in size I made up in viciousness and weapons. I set up alcohol stills, selling raw potato mash to the majority of bars in the city of Toronto. I began using a dump-truck/garbage truck, cleaned out with a false hinge on it, so that we when we would break into clothing and furniture stores, we could load up the truck with the stolen goods. The police never even thought about stopping a garbage truck in the middle of the night!

Then I began to steal transport trailers right from the docks. One of my guys worked on the docks in the company's warehouse and would let me know when there was a trailer filled with some desirable goods. I would snip off the security unit on the back doors of the trailer that was checked when going through the weigh scales on the highway. I would do this by replacing it and punching in a new shipping code punched onto the metal ribbon through another contact in the shipping office who supplied me with the numbers that would allow me to drive the transport trailer to my buyer. We would just leave the full load with her as well as the transport and trailer.

I was barely sixteen. I ran a gang with dozens of members, many of them much older. Why would a twenty year old adult take orders from a fifteen year old kid? The first reason was the "I don't care attitude." I didn't, and I made sure that everybody knew about it. I didn't care who he was, how big he was, how many people he had in his family, how tough he was, or how tough he looked. If he came against me, then he had to be ready to kill me because I was quite prepared to kill him. There was a rage in my belly that removed fear of pain or death when it was triggered. The second reason that people followed me was my discovery of the wonderful world of money. I had a natural talent for making it. I bought my first home when I was fifteen years old and paid $63,000 cash for it. Oh, yes, people can buy homes at fifteen years of age. Money is all that is needed. Money corrupts. I knew that though people may have thought I was garbage, that by having a lot of money, they would call me Sir. I discovered that people worshipped money, and sometimes by extension the people who made it. I discovered that there really was a god and he was on a $100 bill. I discovered that the world revolved around money. I discovered I could buy lawyers. I could do whatever I wanted because money gave me power. I discovered that people would follow me and obey me because I made money and people thought I was something if I had money.

In the 1960's, a group of men approached me. The head of this crew had a "pipeline" for Mexican and Colombian marijuana and had learned how to manufacture LSD or acid. He told me that he wanted to set up a laboratory in Toronto. He said that he needed a good man who knew a lot of people who wanted to make money by moving his product throughout the city.

At seventeen years old, I was to begin an odyssey that would do what most people do in the prison system: live life on the installment plan with twenty-one years of my life spent in the federal penitentiary system of Canada. The only difference between me, and the majority of people going into a prison, was that I actually made the money that I bragged about. The majority of prisoners go to prison from living life below the poverty level. I also began a twenty year night-marish journey as a drug addict. A lifetime of getting strung out on acid, heroin, crystal meth, cocaine and crack cocaine, and whatever else I could get when I couldn't get them.

One year in the late 1960's, I lost three homes, several cars and motorcycles, half ownership of a very large fire extinguisher business, and was reduced to living out of one room, as well as breaking and entering into somebody's house to raid the refrigerator to get food. I had lost it all be-cause of a long binge over two years as a speed freak. Being arrested that year and sent into a maximum security prison actually saved my life.

The lesson it taught me was never to slide that far down the slippery slope of addiction. As a major drug dealer and bandit, I made sure that I never became so sloppy again in my drug use that people wouldn't do business with me. In fact, from that point on, people rarely saw me do drugs. I did them often in secret.

I spent twenty-one and a half years of my life in prison starting at the age of eight. I would go to prison for three to five years at a time and come back out to the street for two or three years at a time, which is what the majority of the prison population does. I fell into the norm and the pat-tern in that way. Over 80% of adult criminals start in juvenile

125

custody, over 90% are functionally illiterate and over 90% have drug or alcohol problems. The majority of them do life on the instalment plan. They come out of prison and recommit crimes until they are caught, and then they go back in. That is the pattern. The only difference with me was that it became high-level crime.

There was very little difference in my behaviour in prison. I spent over six and a half years of my life in solitary confinement. I became a much feared man in every penitentiary in Ontario. In super maximums, I was charged with instigating prison riots and assaulting guards and was investigated for prison murders. I knew not to care. Wasn't that what I was taught, not to care? Hate was equal opportunity, and I hated everybody equally. You see, when life means nothing, then you really don't care about death. When death means nothing, then living means nothing. I had already been drinking since the age of fifteen. I was doing drugs by seventeen-sticking needles in my arm to lose myself in the addict's world of neither being alive nor dead.

I was arrested in 1984 for a laboratory bust having produced about $40 million worth of crystal meth in Glen Sutton in the Eastern Township of the province of Quebec. I had risen in the ranks of drug dealing, to organized criminal circles, a co-leader of one of Canada's most powerful drug organizations. It was to be described in the Royal Canadian Mounted Police journals as the most sophisticated laboratory operation that they had ever investigated. It had international connections with major criminal organizations worldwide.

Regardless of how good I had become as a drug dealer, the RCMP in eighteen months of undercover operatives, wiretaps, and filming, had built a case against us that had our lawyers scrambling to make deals. We only went to court twice, the first time for arraignment and the second several months later. I went to prison once again. I was sentenced to nine years and stripped of everything I owned.

I had never been in the Quebec prisons before, but they were not really too different from prisons anywhere else in Canada. They had separated the twelve of us arrested into five prisons because of the media coverage. I walked into a new prison already known and with celebrity status. A young twenty five year old, a wanna-be biker and weight lifter, must have looked at me and said to himself, "This guy's reputation can't be true. It's got to be over-inflated. This guy can't be as tough as everybody says he is."

Sometimes people make mistakes, sometimes they look at a man and figure that if he doesn't have a whole lot of scars on his face and doesn't look tough then maybe he isn't. This guy made the mistake of deciding he was going to earn a reputation at my expense. I beat him with a three-foot steel table leg. He went to the hospital, and I went to solitary confinement. Again, not unusual.

The warden said, "I'm going to tell you something. They are creating a new super maximum prison in the old St. Vincent de Paul Penitentiary. They are building a prison within a prison – a Special Handling Unit to house one hundred and seventy-five of Canada's toughest and most notorious convicts. You are going there as soon as it is finished. I didn't want you in this prison and you've proven me right."

The warden ordered me to be kept on a secure segregation order (maximum secured confinement within the segregation unit). I was shackled and handcuffed at all times when I left the cell. I was allowed no association with anyone. The only time that the handcuffs were taken off was shower time, while the chains remained on my feet with a chain running up to the chain circling my waist. I was only allowed out of my cell for an hour a day, to walk alone, in a small fenced in walking yard, as well as to shower. No guards or convicts were allowed near me. They fed me through a slot in the door.

No matter how many people talk about prison, they describe it in one word: boring. It has to get boring. Think

127

about it. Prisoners do the same thing everyday, three hundred and sixty- five days a year. Guards tell them when to get up, when to sleep, what to eat, and what to do. In the winter, they can't go outside because the guards are afraid that they will cover themselves in a white sheet in the snow and escape. The only thing that livens things up is worrying about someone stabbing them.

Out of boredom, in the six-by-eight solitary cement cell, I happened one day to look through the door and see a very strange event. In this solitary confinement unit, the steel doors were three and a half inches thick, with bullet proof glass about an inch and a half thick, and below the window, a slot to pass your tray of food through – or to stick your arms through, behind your back, to have handcuffs attached before they opened the door to the cell.

Looking through the window in the door, I was able to see a room off to the side where the bottom half was wood and the top half was glass. That day, I watched the guards bring in a man and strip-search him. I thought this was very unusual. It wasn't the fact that he was being strip-searched. In many prisons, prisoners are often strip-searched three or four times a day. It was a common occurrence, especially for violent prisoners who had carried a weapon or drugs on them. They did it to harass us. In fact, they usually try to do it with women guards just to make it more embarrassing. So, it wasn't the fact that this man was being strip-searched that drew my attention but the fact that he was smiling and he wasn't a convict!

All my life I have studied human nature. For me, it was a matter of survival on the streets as a young man and later survival in the crime world – to judge whether or not somebody was a danger to me. I felt that I had become an expert at judging human nature, but this was the first time I had seen anybody humiliated and insulted who smiled through it! I found this very unusual. It got my attention. Out of curiosity, I asked one of the cleaners who the man was, only to find out that he was a volunteer.

He was a volunteer who wouldn't get paid for going into the prison – or into the solitary unit! He came in twice a week and he got strip-searched. The fool! I was angry because I couldn't figure him out. What the heck is it with this guy! I'd watch him go to the cells, hand out a few magazines, and talk a few minutes with each convict. Then he would come around the range to my side, and I would be in front of my door practicing my best Clint Eastwood snarl – glaring at him through the window in the door as he passed by – and he'd just smile at me! Oh, I was so angry with him. One of the cleaners told me that he was a Christian, and that the magazines he was handing out were Christian magazines. Then I knew he was nuts—a Christian!

Solitary confinement is a place where prisoners often go crazy. Frequently the riot squad needs to come and contain a convict who is losing it, smashing up his cell, going to commit suicide, or slashing up. Often tear gas is used against him. People start running head first into walls. It gets pretty nutty in there, and they did not want this guy in there – they made it very difficult for him. The volunteer disrupted the routine, and maybe he would see a few things that he wasn't supposed to see, but somehow he had gotten permission, and he was there twice a week.

The warden came to me one day to personally tell me that I was being shipped out on the next load going to St. Vincent de Paul Penitentiary. As soon as he told me, there became only one thing on my mind and it was that little man. I waited for him to come in and do his rounds. I watched him go through his routine. When he stopped at the front of my door, this time, instead of letting him go by, I smashed it as hard as I could. I had learned a long time ago that the best form of defence was an offence. It startled him and put him on the defensive. He jumped in the air and I started screaming at him through the slot in the door, "You're nuts! You got to be nuts! You come in here, you let the guards humiliate you and treat you like dirt. They insult you, but you come in twice a week and hand out magazines and speak to the garbage in here who nobody wants to speak to. You're brain-damaged. I know. I am an expert. You are without a doubt, brain-damaged!"

He paused for a second and looked at me. By this time, I was frothing at the mouth. I had really worked myself up and was going to give this guy a what-for, but he just calmly looked at me and said, "You may be right." Now let me tell you something. If you ever want to stop an argument in a hurry, just agree with the person who is arguing with you. I did not know what to say from that point on. He just said that I might be right. What did he mean, I may be right? He spoke calmly: "I happen to be a Christian. I happen to believe that God never made garbage and I happen to believe that Jesus Christ died for everyone, including you. I happen to believe that if you were the last person on this earth and there was no one else left, that Jesus Christ would come and die for you. That's how important you are."

"I know all about you—everybody knows about you. You are one of the most infamous convicts to walk in and out of prison. I know that. I know about your background. I know about all the stuff you've done. You know the guards talk about you as soon as you come to a prison because you've broken guards' jaws and you have instigated riots. No matter where you go, they talk about how crazy you are, about your background, and all the gang stuff. You want to know something? All of those things are cop-outs for the bad choices you have made."

"I choose to believe that everybody is created equal and I choose to believe that everybody is created in excellence. From that point on, it's the choices we make in life. You choose to either believe that you are an animal who walks on two legs – a fluke of nature with no purpose and no soul or you can choose to believe that there is a Creator and you are a creation – with great value, purpose and with a soul. If you so choose to believe that you are a creation rather than a thing – then the outcome to your life is based on the choices you make with it. The most important choice in the world, as I see it, is to understand that you are a creation of God and that His Son, Jesus Christ died for you so that you would know salvation and how to live life."

He then thrust a magazine through the slot in the cell door. He left me stunned. I just kind of looked at this guy. I was angry. How dare he confront me that way! How dare he tell me that the majority of my life was my fault! How dare he do that? Didn't he know that I was a product of rape, abused as a kid, lived through training school horrors, and lived on the streets?

Later on that night while eating dinner, I looked at the Christian magazine that I had thrown into the corner – Jubilee by Prison Fellowship Canada, and staring back at me on the front cover was a good friend of mine by the name of Roy Hill, one of the toughest men I had ever met in prison. Constantly in and out of prison, a professional bodyguard, Roy had beaten up police officers four or five at a time, and here he was on the cover of a Christian magazine!

Yeah, right, another one bites the dust, gone soft in the head – burnt out, too much time in prison I thought to myself. Yet it was Roy Hill. I knew him. I knew how mean and tough he was. I couldn't stop wondering what the article had to say, so I decided to read it. I mean, it wasn't like I had a lot of other things to do anyway. Roy spoke of his life in the article, a tough life as a child, alcoholism and drugs as a teenager, anger and pain, hate and rage, and many years of his life in prison beginning as a juvenile. Not a whole lot different than my own life or many convicts' lives. Then Roy said something that I couldn't stop thinking about. It kept coming into my head late at night during the next few months. In the last sentence in the article, Roy stated, "For the first time in my life, I've come to know peace of mind and freedom." A

131

few days later, I was transferred to the Special Handling Unit in St. Vincent DePaul Penitentiary.

In any super maximum-security prison, the one thing you can count on is a lot of cell time – usually twenty-three hours a day. You have a lot of time to think, and I just couldn't stop thinking about what that volunteer had said to me – that he had the audacity to say that to me! I also knew that what he said he believed because I watched him do exactly what he believed twice a week. I knew he believed it. otherwise he would not have done what he did. I knew that he believed that what he said was the truth, at least as far as he was concerned.

What Roy Hill also said in the article was driving me nuts. What was freedom and peace of mind anyway? I couldn't get it out of my mind. Roy Hill's words in the article and the words and actions of Jim Yorgey, the Christian volunteer, somehow rang true. He hadn't preached at me, hadn't Bible thumped, but didn't do the 'oh, poor you' either. That truth was challenging the "I don't care attitude" and the hate, but I wasn't ready for it. I knew that my course in life was set and that it was too late to change it.

This new super-max prison in Quebec was very weird: weird food, weird events, a lot of killings, and a lot of cell time. I had grown quite close to a young man from Hamilton who was in a cell beside me. We often played chess and cards through the bars in the front of our cells on the floor of the catwalk. Being side by side, our cells were often opened at the same time to go to pick up our supper trays, to go for our showers, and to go to the yard for our exercise hour. Glen had robbed three pizza shops with an unloaded shotgun. He stole a total of three hundred and fifty dollars to buy crystal meth, and he received ten years in federal prison as a sentence.

He first went to Millhaven Penitentiary, and while in the Reception Unit, a guy raped him, so he got a homemade prison knife and stabbed the guy. Since there were only two of them and one guy had a knife sticking out of his chest, it was obvious as to who had put the knife in him. They added another ten years to his prison sentence and sent him to the super-max in Quebec, in the cell next to mine. He was nineteen-years-old, doing twenty years in jail. I grew to like this kid.

As time went by, he told me his life story. His mother had been a prostitute and he had half a dozen half-brothers and sisters. He had gone from foster home to foster home, from juvenile prison to juvenile prison. He had struck out on his own at the age of fifteen after being sexually abused at one of the foster-care homes. He got involved with drugs and then crime to support his addiction. He had gotten really 'strung out' on crystal meth and committed the robberies to get money to buy more. He hadn't wanted to hurt anyone so had never loaded the shotgun, but the police hadn't believed him when he told them that. I knew that during the time period that he was strung out and committing this crime that the crystal meth he had been using had come from my dealers and from my laboratory operation.

Maybe because of his sad life story, or maybe because I felt a little responsible for his circumstances, I felt that I needed to take him under my wing and help him along. I began to tutor him with advice that I knew he would need to make it during the next twenty years in the 'insane asylum' called the prison system of Canada. I said, "Listen, in order to survive kid, you've got to not care. You have to care less than everyone else. You have to make sure everybody knows that you don't care. You got to not care about what's happening to you or around you. You've got to be willing to sacrifice your body. That's the only way you are going to survive." Well, he cared so little that he ended up tearing up his sheets and hanging himself.

I had seen death before, many times during my lifetime, but Glen's impacted me like no other. I realized I had given him bad advice because the ultimate not caring is dying by your own hand. I also knew that I had spent most of my life as a drug dealer dealing death to kids like Glen. I wondered if Glen would have gotten himself put into prison for such a desperate crime if he hadn't gotten strung out on the crystal meth that came from my dealers. What if my drugs hadn't been on the street! I then decided for the first time in my life that I was going to commit suicide. I was disgusted with myself, and I decided I was going to do it the hardest way possible: I was going to starve myself to death. Growing up as a street child, food was very important to me and I wanted to punish myself. I wanted to make my death slow and painful.

A week went by. I wasn't eating and I wasn't leaving my cell. I was depressed and all I did was sleep. A friend that I had known for many years, through many other prisons, stopped in front of my cell and began to speak with me. He said, "Listen, I'm really worried about you. You know, the kid beside you commits suicide, you're not coming out of your cell, I don't see you taking any meals, you're not working out on the weights or the heavy bag, and, you know....."

I replied, "Yeah, you're right. I got all these questions, but I haven't got the answers. I just got no answers anymore. I mean, just nothing means anything. Man, am I messed."

Then he said, "You know, I have an answer."

"You've got an answer."

"Yeah."

"So what's the answer?"

"I'm not telling you."

Frustrated, I demanded, "So, what do you mean, you're not telling me? What are you, a wise guy?"

He said, "I know you. I've known you all my life since we were kids together. You are one of the most stubborn men I've ever met. You are hard-headed. You do everything the hard way. If I give you the answer, you're not going to accept it. You need to find it out for yourself."

"Alright, where do I find it?"

"I'm going to the chapel. Come with me."

I retorted, "Chapel, are you nuts? Go to the chapel? Last time I was in a chapel I got my jaw broke. I'm not going to chapel."

"Now wait a minute. You're trying to starve yourself to death and you don't want to go to chapel?"

"Alright, what do you do at the chapel?"

"We sing songs."

I said, "I've heard you sing. You sing like a frog. I'm not going to chapel. What else do you do?"

"We have coffee and doughnuts."

I was not impressed or interested! "Yeah, right."

He said, "I'm serious. You want answers and you're not even sure of the questions. I've got the answer to the only important question as far as I am concerned. I'm doing a double life sentence, I'm going to die in prison, and if it was the only way I could find that answer, I would have it all happen over again the same way in order to find it. It's that important." When somebody tells you that, you want to pay attention. I did.

"Okay, tell the screw to crack the door, and let's go." I went down there, but for the first two or three times I didn't talk to anybody. I just looked and listened.

Then I began speaking to one of the volunteers who came to the evening group. This fellow's name was Larry Duguay and he and his wife Sandy always came in together. He worked as a janitor and gave up time to come in twice a week. Sandy sang during Sunday service and often their five daughters joined them for special events. They were honest, hardworking folk who gave up the most valuable thing in life, time, to spend it with convicts like myself. I listened and I learned – and my questions began to be answered.

Nine months later, I became a Christian. On December 25, 1985, at two o'clock in the morning, I got down on my knees in that super maximum-security penitentiary and invited Jesus Christ into my life. Prison gates didn't spring open, the cell bars didn't melt, the walls didn't rumble and fall down, and blinding lights didn't shine down upon me. Yet somewhere in the pit of my stomach, I knew I would never be the same again. Deep inside of me, something had changed. I knew that it was real.

It then took me seven weeks to do the most courageous thing I had ever done. I prayed the sinner's prayer with Larry and made a public declaration letting him think that it was the first time I was doing it. I had already made my deal with God all by myself. The interesting thing was that when I made that deal, I was smoking dope, carrying a homemade prison knife up one sleeve, and swearing like a sailor on shore leave after a year at sea. I still thought in the old way of settling problems with violence and calling the guards names as I still thought of guards and prison personnel as the enemy.

The reality of it is that we are told in Scripture, "Therefore, if anyone is in Christ, he is a new creation; the old has gone, the new has come!" (2 Corinthians 5:17) It is a process of change. We are told quite specifically to come to Him and give Him our burdens. He tells us to take His load upon us, and He will take ours. His load is easy: "Come to me, all you who are weary and burdened, and I will give you rest. Take my yoke (partnership) upon you and learn from me, for I am gentle and humble in heart, and you will find rest for your souls. For my yoke (partnership) is easy and my burden is light" (Matthew 11:28-30). Your heart is changed and now the process begins, empowered by your faith and His teaching, to begin to change the way you think and live.

I don't do drugs anymore. That ended in 1986 when I began to live my life as a Christian in that super maximum security prison. I spent twenty years as a drug addict – thirteen years as an intravenous drug user and another seven smoking and snorting cocaine. In the seventies, I gave myself so much crystal meth that my blood almost crystallized.

I couldn't come down. For me, it was always a contest to see how many drugs I could do and what the limit was before I could die. It was always to the extreme.

I was released from prison August 26, 1988. Twelve years later, in the year 2000, the Government of Canada gave me a full national pardon, setting a new precedent in the history of Canada – in answer to a request from Crime Stoppers personnel including police chiefs and RCMP inspectors throughout North America! Nobody linked with organized crime, with my criminal record of violence, armed robberies, violence in prison, massive drug use, massive drug dealing, and just about every crime imaginable has been pardoned. The Government of Canada gave me a full national pardon in recognition of the full and complete change in my life.

From a grade five education in 1986, I received my first college diploma in 1989, my first university degree in 1991, and an Honours degree with a double major in sociology and social work in 1993. I graduated on the Dean's Honour List from the University of Waterloo for outstanding achievement—not bad for somebody who is brain-damaged!

Reverend Ian Stanley, the then Director of Prison Fellowship Canada arranged for me to speak before the Legislative Assembly of Canada in 1990 for ten minutes on the issue of cocaine addiction and ineffective treatment methods. They were sending addicts for treatment costing millions of dollars, and they were coming back and going right back into crack and coke. I told these people, "I'll give you the answer for addictions in two words: Jesus Christ. I'll give you the answer for prison in two words: Jesus Christ. Jesus Christ sets prisoners free from the bondage and the chains that they have wrapped around themselves. That is fact."

I stand here today as a living testimony to Jesus Christ in my own life. Everything that I am and everything that I do is because of Jesus Christ and the power of God to change lives from the inside out. Jesus Christ changed my life. I'm still the product of rape, born in an abandoned building to a young mother. I'm still a half-breed, a bastard, and I'm still a kid who was brought up in the inner city, on the streets. I am still the person who was in juvenile custody at age eight and who spent twenty-one years of my life in prison with six years in solitary confinement. That's all the same. The only difference is that today I am a Christian. Jesus Christ became part of my life. I made Him part of my lifestyle. That is the reality.

Jesus Christ doesn't take your past or your present into consideration. He doesn't say to us: *You know, you have to be good enough for me to accept you. You have to come to me without drugs and alcohol, be well educated and be from a good family.* Rather He says to us: *Come to Me as you are – a sinner. Come to Me with that garbage. Come to Me with your 'I don't care attitude,' with your hate and rage, with your sexual abuse and physical abuse, and with your hopelessness and pain. Come to Me with it, and I'll take it onto Me. I'll deal with it, I'll work with it, and I'll heal you from it. I'll give you the strength of the Holy Spirit in your life so that you will able to walk the walk and can live your life in freedom. I will begin the process in you in order for you to live a new life.*

When Jesus Christ came to earth, He said, "I have come to proclaim freedom for the prisoner"(Luke 4:18). We need to understand that prison isn't just concrete, steel, iron bars and guards. Prisons are things that we lock ourselves in. Whether it's envy, greed, hate, jealousy, gambling, drugs, pornography, or sex, we lock ourselves into those prisons. Jesus Christ came to say: *I will set you free from those prisons. I will give you peace of mind, I will give you freedom to live your life. Most of all, I will give you the strength to break your chains through the Holy Spirit.*

Yes, I was an evil man. Don't ever forget that the things that I did in my life were evil. There are many people who grew up in the Inner City, and many people who grew up in juvenile custody, and many bad things happened to them, but they didn't resort to the evil that I did. I was evil in my actions and I was evil by choice, but Jesus Christ delivered me from the malice, the chains, those prisons, and that mind set, and the Christian volunteers held me to it. They showed me by example in their walk. They challenged me in my way of thinking. When I got out of prison and went to live with a Christian family, they did the same thing in challenging me. I needed to immerse myself in a Christian community, break away from my past and walk the walk.

We, however, need to understand the power of the Holy Spirit to change lives. My life change is a witness to that power – to the power of Jesus Christ to change lives, to protect lives, and to give meaning to life. Without Jesus Christ, there is no meaning to life. If there is no God, then we are nothing more than animals that walk on two legs. We are either one or the other: created in the image of a creator or animals. Historians say that Jesus Christ is real. Nobody ever denies that is a fact. The only people who deny Jesus Christ in any way deny that He was the Son of God.

I leave this message with you: I was a gang leader, and whenever I got arrested, my gang split. Jesus Christ got crucified and his gang also split. They went into hiding for fear of their lives. Yet, His gang had to have seen Him resurrected, otherwise they were all insane or idiots because every one of His apostles came out of hiding to tell all that would listen that Jesus Christ was the Son of God. That He had returned from the dead. Every one of His gang because of that died violent, ugly deaths in the form of crucifixion upside down, shot full of arrows and stoned because of their beliefs. His gang wouldn't do that for a lie. It would only do it if Jesus was the truth.

I know human nature.

I know that Jesus Christ is real because His disciples carried the gospel message at risk of death and imprisonment. No one does that unless it is real. I know Jesus Christ is real because I wouldn't be here today without Him, and that's a fact. My life wouldn't be the way it is today without Jesus Christ, and that's a fact that even the Government of Canada recognizes. The reality of the power of Jesus Christ and the Holy Spirit in our lives is fact.

For any of you reading this who don't know Jesus Christ personally – why not? What are you scared of? What is it that you are holding onto that you can't let go? Why is your pain so comforting? Why is your hate so comforting? Why is your self-doubt so comforting that you won't let it go? That was my biggest battle. Jesus Christ is real. Jesus Christ changes lives. Jesus Christ will take your burdens onto Himself and give you the strength to live your life. If you haven't a relationship with Jesus Christ, you need to decide now. It is simple. All I did was ask Jesus Christ into my life to be my Lord and Saviour. I did it all by myself in a super maximum security penitentiary cell, but I didn't do it with my mouth, and I didn't do it with my head. I did it with my heart. He says that when we open our hearts, we allow Him into our hearts; then He will change our lives forever. He did, and He does.

Postscript

We were commanded by Jesus Christ to deliver, in the ministry of reconciliation, the Gospel of Jesus Christ to all corners of the earth, and one of the corners of the earth is called prison. It's an alien country. It is a godless country filled with pain and hate and desperation. It is a country filled with poverty—poverty of spirit. It is a country filled with hopelessness and pain, and yet it is a country that can be redeemed by the blood of Jesus Christ that was already shed for us. Serge LeClerc is proud to be working with a ministry that delivers on that call: New Life Prison Ministry (www.nlpm.com).

Serge LeClerc

Serge LeClerc is presently the Director of Teen Challenge Saskatchewan in Saskatoon, (www.tcsk.org). Teen Challenge is an Interdenominational Christian Ministry operating over six hundred faith-based residential substance abuse treatment centres in eighty two countries beginning in 1957 by David Wilkerson in the inner city of New York. It incorporates education, work and life skills, counselling, and moral and lifestyle discipleship for youth and young adults with life problems caused by addictions.

Serge has been the past Executive Director of Prairie Hope Ministries, Saskatoon, Saskatchewan, the Assistant

Executive Director of Turning Point Ministries, Co-founder of Rocklyn Academy, a private school for troubled girls, Head of Counselling Services of the Creative Center for Learning and Development, a private school for troubled boys, Director of Maranatha Ministries, and President of Career 7 Associates – all in Ontario, Canada. As a motivational speaker and seminar lecturer, he has spoken to well over 3,000,000 people throughout North America, especially on behalf of Crime Stoppers International. He founded and was the Chapter Director of Kitchener-Waterloo Prison Fellowship Canada. He has appeared many times on television on Focus on the Family and 100 Huntley Street. His personal web site is (www.sergetalks.com)

Chapter Six

TO HELL
AND
BACK

The Life
of
John Anderson

To Hell and Back

My life has been marked by the continual, brooding fear of horrors yet to come. I know what it is like to wake every day dreading the thought of being alive, terrified of the future and revolted by my own state. To those who themselves may know something of that experience I dedicate this recounting of my own story.

It Begins

I was born in the drug culture of the sixties, and my parents were both products of that movement. My father was in his early twenties and mother was still a teenager when they got married. My mother was an Ojibwa girl who grew up in an environment of squalor and alcohol abuse, moving from reservation to reservation as a child. My father had a glamorous job as a trainer with racehorses, which made him travel between Canada and the U.S. frequently, going from racetrack to racetrack. I guess this life must have seemed very appealing to my mother who had only experienced abuse and desperation in her life. I was told that my father took her away from all the abuse. When I look back now, I think she exchanged one type of abuse for another.

My father had come from lower-middle class parents who were hard working and honest. My father's family had conservative, respectable values. From old photos of him I notice an air of arrogance and rebelliousness in my father's eyes, and I think it was that attitude that led him astray later in his life. My father's arrogant pride and rebelliousness coupled with my mother's desperate childhood was probably the volatile mix that eventually propelled them into drug addiction and life without borders.

I recall many parties and gatherings at our house when I was a child. The memories are rather blurry now, but I do remember that there was rarely a sense of security in our home and things were always in a state of getting worse.

Though I was not aware of what kind of drugs my parents did, I knew instinctively that they were doing "bad things" behind closed doors. Their marriage spiralled out of control as they fought more and more, and yelling eventually turned to physical abuse. My siblings and I went into foster care for over half a year. My older brother was put in a separate foster home across the city, and my sister and I would only see him on occasional family visits.

Our foster parents were never really suited to care for the fragile, broken children we were. As a result of their lack of skills, my sister and I suffered emotional abuse. Heaped on top of this was the ongoing damage that my mother caused us from a distance. She promised us regularly that we would be going home the next week. My sister and I would count the minutes waiting for the day to arrive when we would go home. That day would come and go, but we would wait in vain for hours choking on our tears just waiting for my mother and father to come and take us home. Eventually, we simply lost faith and became hardened to the reality that we were abandoned to these strangers. I really believe that this experience as a child, helped to harden my heart and cause me to distrust everything. At nine years old, I came to the realization that I was truly alone.

My sister and I were eventually reunited with our parents and older brother to try again, but I recall thinking that it seemed like my parents were trying too hard to hold it together. Not long after, my parents had another son, and a daughter soon after that. My father spent more and more time away from home, and when my parents were together they would fight constantly. My mother began to decline, becoming extremely irritable for little or no apparent reason, and would take it out on me and my other four siblings. Eventually we grew to live in fear of the consequences for any mistake – no matter how small. Violence escalated in our home. The only relief from the growing dysfunction all around us kids was the comfort we received from each other. My father was rarely around, and when he did come home it was only to sleep; then he was gone again. This left my oldest brother, who was just a child himself, burdened with the responsibility to raise us all later in life, the damage of this became apparent in his life.

Food was always scarce at our house but it began to get scary when we would go to bed hungry and then to school the next day without breakfast. I became very good at stealing chocolate bars and candy to feed myself. Other kids that I knew stole candy and chocolate as a treat, but I learned very quickly that stealing sardines or packaged meat was a sure thing because nobody expects a kid to steal real food.

I recall a time when my mother spent several days in the basement neglecting us and we were getting very hungry. My brothers, sisters and I were at the top of the stairs leading to the basement crying because we were so hungry. I remember feeling that something was terribly wrong because my mother spent long hours in that basement and only briefly came up the stairs to yell at us to stay away. Finally, after we were crying for so long at the basement door my mother got angry and forced me to go into the basement while forbidding the rest of the kids to go downstairs. There, my mother demanded that I watch her stick a needle in her arm as she screamed, "this is what you wanted to see so badly!" I was only about seven years old. I did not know what the needle was, but to me it all somehow seemed very evil. There are moments in every person's life that help to define them and ultimately shape him or her. For me, I think seeing my mother stick a needle in her arm was the final message that told me once and for all, nothing could be trusted again.

I did not hate my mother for this, I felt ashamed for her. I felt deeply sorry for her. I started to understand why she was so angry and frustrated all the time. She hated herself. There was no way that she wanted to live this way and I knew from that moment on, that my mother was a slave. I began to understand that this bondage was the real reason for the violence and the pain in my family. Sadly, I came to believe that this was our lot in life.

Every night we would see images on TV from the war in Vietnam. I would force myself to think about the suffering of Vietnamese children, and the terrible fear they must have experienced with constant violence and killing around them.

Even though those children were far away and suffered much more than I, I felt a strange connection to them. Even though there were no dead bodies lying all around, people around me were dying all the time. I watched my mother and father slowly kill themselves everyday. I watched them destroy everything and everyone around them bit by bit.

By the late sixties and into the seventies, we lived in government housing projects in Scarborough in the suburbs of Toronto. I remember that most of my friends from the projects were suffering from the same dysfunctional family situations as I was, to one degree or another. However, outside of the projects it was a different story. I recall going to a lower middle class school and trying to fit in with other children from more fortunate homes. It became painfully obvious to me that they lived very different lives than I did. I saw them as enjoying stable loving families, nice homes, and warm meals every night. I never felt resentment towards any of my friends from outside the projects. I just felt worse for us. When a person sees others enjoying life without suffering, that makes the suffering far deeper.

I guess I started to see most people as being different from me, especially those from the other side of the tracks. I never really felt good enough to want to accomplish anything, because I saw myself as a lower being, one with the cards stacked against me. As I got older, the feelings of worthlessness seemed to be confirmed by every passing day. I could not relate to other kids my age, and schooling seemed useless to me. I felt disengaged; cut off. I know now that much of my time spent daydreaming in school was due to the fact that I was always trying to find meaning to it all. My whole childhood was spent searching for some sort of meaning to my life. The funny thing was that I had no direction for my questions, and in fact, I didn't even know what the questions really were.

I started to skip school regularly and developed a blatant disregard for any type of authority. I don't think I was angry, I just didn't care because I didn't think anything really mattered to me. I began to feel like I was the master of my own destiny, and I did what I wanted. Neither one of my parents really had much control over me and I think their efforts to discipline me seemed too hypocritical even for them. So I proceeded into a life of petty crime and any kind of abuse that appealed to me.

I got more and more into a life of petty crime as a juvenile. I recall a time after one of my parent's drug parties, I stole a couple of joints off my mother and tried to get high on pot, but for some reason it had no affect on me. My first arrest came after I was hanging around with one of my friends from the projects and we decided that we would like to run away and go on a crime spree. We hitchhiked around for a couple of days stealing out of stores and breaking into homes. Eventually we became extremely hungry, and we broke into a farmhouse with no one home and ate what we could find in the fridge. In the kitchen there was a .22 rifle and a machete leaning against the wall, so we took them and went to the barn. We were planning on camping in the bush so we caught a small pig to slaughter it for food. We took off into the fields to butcher the pig. As we sat in a clearing trying to figure out how we were going to butcher the pig, the police came from all directions with their guns drawn on us. I wound up going to a juvenile detention center for a couple weeks and had much time to think about the direction my life was taking, I had no answers. I was only eleven or twelve years old.

I was placed on probation as a juvenile and introduced to the first person to have a significant impact on my thinking, my probation officer. She was the first person to offer the suggestion that my life had value. She spent many long hours with me and showed a genuine interest. Through small acts of unconditional love, and long, meaningful conversations, she showed me that she loved me. My mind started to open up to the possibility that maybe there was significant meaning to life.

The Road Down

Then my whole world fell apart. In the late summer of 1972 after a tremendously violent fight between my parents, my mother left to go on one of her binges and never returned. I remember driving with my father in his taxi as we went looking for my mother in downtown Toronto, and I saw him cry for the first time. When I saw him cry for the first time (and the only time since), it broke my heart because I knew why he was crying. Everything was way out of hand. He knew that his wife had left him with five kids, and she wasn't coming back.

My mother did call the house, and she arranged for me and my older brother to meet her downtown. From there everything becomes a blur. For a while, my older brother and I lived with my mother on the streets, moving from one junkie's apartment to another. All the time my heart was getting harder and harder and trust was all gone. I went into survival mode. I began to live off my instincts.

Then word came to us that my younger brother and sisters had been taken into foster care. My older brother was eventually found by the Children's Aid Society and taken into care. I was able to elude the Children's Aid until they caught up with me when I was thirteen. My mother had received word from my father that the police were looking for me because my probation officer had not seen me in some time. I turned myself in, and went into foster care for the third time in my life.

By then I had a huge chip on my shoulder and a fearless attitude – but really it was to hide the fear that was deep within. I did not trust a soul. In the foster home I found other kids with an attitude like mine. I quickly made friends, but at the same time I continued to rebel against all authority in my life. My new foster parents were pretty tough but I wore them down eventually as I continually skipped school to find trouble downtown at every opportunity.

I was bounced out of the group home in order to live with a young professional couple that had a nice home in a more affluent neighborhood in the inner city. I did not particularly like the new home with all the rules, but I liked the fact that it was closer to the city, and I had a genuine sense that maybe this could be a chance for change. I did try briefly to improve my attitude, and my foster parents did have a significant impact on my thinking. In retrospect, I see they made genuine efforts to care for me, though I was not ready to realize it then. I actually felt the most comfortable with these people, even though I challenged them at every turn. I would continually steal from them, manipulate and lie to them, but their response to me was always one of unconditional love, understanding and acceptance.

Yet I was struggling with the darkness within. I lived a double life. On one hand, I took great interest in the opportunities that these people provided. For example, my foster father was a journalist for a major Toronto newspaper and had a great zeal for things like ecology and the out doors. As a result I was introduced to many wonderful experiences that encouraged and challenged me. I loved going camping in the far north in the summer, and one year we did a six-week cross-country road trip. I was exposed to many experiences that would have never been available to me in the projects. But on the other hand, I was challenged by temptations that seemed too great for me to pass up. I was never able to shake the deep feelings of inadequacy or the desire to take what wasn't mine. I recall pulling many break-and-enters, and never got caught. This led me to feel almost invincible – a true criminal. For two years I lived this way.

Eventually, the lie that I was living got out of control and my foster parents started to see me for what I really was. One time I was caught in the act of stealing money from them and it all came to a head. When they realized the depth of my deception they were disappointed and hurt at first, but I think they soon came to see me as a threat to their young family. I really WAS a threat, and I knew it. In my private moments I agonized over my inability to control my dark impulses; and I knew that I was hurting these people who loved me so much. Secretly, I was deeply ashamed.

My deception and frustration grew so bad that I think I secretly sabotaged the placement in the home because I knew that I could never really offer these caring people anything good. I had a sense that I could never live up to their level. So I was sent to another group home. I lashed out in anger because I felt like I was being abandoned again; but deep down, I knew that I had to leave.

The next home I went to was a group home for teenaged boys. At first I was surprised at how quickly I was able settle in to this new environment. I think my heart was becoming so calloused that it didn't really matter where I was because I knew that I could adapt to just about anything. I was fourteen, I was in high school, and it was becoming harder to stay on top of my studies with all of the drugs and partying. I now had access to a steady supply of drugs through the other boys in the group home and connections at school. Everyone I knew was always high on something. Smoking pot became the norm, and I started to experiment with harder drugs like acid and MDA. I had a growing sense that things were getting too far gone and I was afraid of how this was all going to end for me.

I tried desperately to keep myself from giving up on school, but I simply could not deal with it. I dropped out of grade nine after three months. My future looked bleak. I continued living in silent, debilitating fear of the future, and tried getting menial jobs here and there; but there was not much available for a scared, uneducated fifteen year old. I worked for a while at odd jobs, and convinced the Children's Aid to let me have my own apartment, a one-room dump. Now I felt really alone.

I kicked around for two years at jobs here and there that never lasted more than a couple weeks or months at the most. All the while, the Children's Aid was supporting me. The partying was a way of life, while fear and depression haunted me constantly. The only relief I ever found was by getting high or drunk. However, even getting high was no longer offering me any solace because the hopelessness of my situation seemed to intensify when I got stoned.

Then, one day, the light went on! Somehow I reasoned with myself that I needed to get away and cut loose from all of the bad history and failure that I had experienced in my life. I needed to do something radical or I would surely waste away and eventually die in this situation. So I decided that I needed to go far away and find a life for myself where no body knew me. I needed to find some place of opportunity. Western Canada had lots of jobs, and there had to be a place for me there. At the very least, I would have a great adventure and force myself to grow up and be a man! I would give all my possessions away (which didn't amount to much anyway) and hitchhike out west. I would make my own opportunity or die trying. Two weeks after I decided my course, I left with a knapsack on my back, two hundred bucks in my pocket, and a bag of weed for the road.

Trying to Make a Change

I was seventeen. I found a steady ride just outside of Thunder Bay, and made it all the way to the Rockies in three days. I was quick to find myself a job as a pot-washer at the Banff Springs Hotel, and with my last five bucks I went to the nearest watering hole. I quickly discovered that most of the people living in Banff were from somewhere else, and many were from Ontario or down east. I easily fit in to this group of people because we all seemed to be looking for the same thing – a new beginning.

I met a girl at that bar. We stayed in Banff together for a couple of months. Banff was a party town and very few people ever settle down there for too long. We moved to Calgary where jobs seemed plentiful and the rent wasn't too bad. We lived in western Canada for three years and had some pretty good jobs, by Toronto standards. I think the distraction of work in Calgary, where I made some good money, kept me pretty busy and drew me out of a life of crime temporarily. However, the job boom in Calgary eventually dried up and I found myself wondering how I was going to survive. My girlfriend (who was destined to be my first wife) got pregnant, and I had to make a move. I convinced her to stay with some friends while I invested all of our limited money in drugs to peddle in northern Alberta. Within four months I had blown all our money on partying and survival. I went back to Calgary, packed up my pregnant girlfriend and headed back to Ontario to try it all again.

We got married. By then I was no longer a teenager. I guess that I felt more mature, with some experience under my belt, a new wife and a child. I was motivated to find work wherever I could and do my best to make things right. But I always knew my first marriage was one of convenience. I could not settle down within my heart, and I continued to look for ways out.

We moved to Oshawa, and I did find good work and good pay; I worked in the maintenance department of a big

153

heavy metal stamping plant that made car bumpers for the big North American car manufacturers. There I developed some drug connections through people I knew. I became a regular supplier of small time drugs like marijuana, hash and their derivatives, hash oil and so on. At the time, I did not sell large quantities; but I did keep the boys at the plant supplied as best I could.

Meanwhile, my life was spinning out of control again. My wife was becoming restless with all my craziness and partying. Soon I was in bad situations with other women. My wife endured a little over a year of my reckless habits and my womanizing ways. I got to the point where I didn't care who saw me with strange women. Eventually my wife had had enough, and she left one day and took my first-born son with her. That gave me one moment of clarity, where I really saw myself and the damage I had done. I agonized over and over about my inability to be a good loving father and husband, but I knew I did not have the inner fortitude to be that kind of person. I had a major breakdown, but it only lasted for about a week.

I continued to work at the plant but I only held my job by a thread. Now that I was free from any marital respon-sibilities, I was looking for ways to make it big in the drug world. I had a few connections, and attempted to smuggle drugs from Jamaica. That almost got me murdered. I was down there with a girl I did not know, to try to transport some hash oil and cocaine back into Canada. While we were stay-ing at the main drug connection's house, he discovered that the girl I was with was not my girlfriend, and he got nervous. He thought we were drug agents. I could not sleep for three days while I heard them talking about how they were go-ing to deal with us. I had heard about others who had been killed by this guy, and I knew he was very capable. At night I kept a six-foot bamboo stick and a machete under my bed, as I waited in fear. Finally I could not take it any longer, so

I confronted him alone with the machete. I threatened to slit his throat, and I told him that I wasn't prepared to die and it would be nothing for me to kill him where he sat. Somehow this got some respect from him, and he changed his mind about us. Secretly, I wanted to call the whole deal off. But the Chief of Police for the district personally supplied us with drugs – just enough to make a small profit and pay for the trip. He actually gave us the option of having the dope brought to us on the plane, by a policeman! How ironic is that? I recall thinking it would be smarter just to get out of there. But I took the drugs.

During the flight back to Canada I overheard a couple of men sitting a few rows behind me discussing the various details of my plans for the trip! Horrified, I turned around to see three men (obviously detectives) sitting together, grinning smugly at me. I was absolutely terrified, and I knew that the moment I got off the plane I was going to be busted and go straight to jail.

But I caught a break. As the plane was landing, a passenger had a heart attack near the rear of the plane. Emergency paramedics and police were all over the plane within seconds of landing. They were all in the rear of the plane attending to the heart attack victim; passengers were quickly ushered off the plane by the aircrew, in a chaotic way. I slipped into the crowd. As we all lined up to go through the Customs check, it seemed like hours as I waited for my turn to be processed. I watched the mirrored walls in the customs area, thinking that at any minute I'd be caught. But I went through without a hitch, and to my surprise and utterly confused relief, nobody approached me in the airport lobby, on the drive home, or in the days and months to follow. I can only guess that the police were watching me, but were after bigger fish.

Not long after my failed smuggling attempts my father happened to come back into my life. I hadn't seen him in over seven years but somehow we reconnected and we began to visit each other from time to time. By this time, my father himself was very well connected in the drug world, and was into some pretty large quantities of methamphetamine. You don't make "meth" in large quantities without a well-equipped lab and access to special chemicals. This meant my father had some pretty powerful connections in the underworld.

I got my father to hook me up with deals here and there from time to time, but it was all petty stuff, and anything I did with my father up to that point was minor league. But one day my father and his buddy showed up at my apartment in Oshawa. He said he knew that I was "solid," but he needed to confirm my loyalty. I wanted to be a heavy hitter. I wanted to be in the big leagues, so when he asked if he could stash some dope at my place I had no problem with it. With a stash under my sink worth about $40,000 to any dealer and at least twice that much on the street, I was taking a stupid risk. The value in money was not really the issue; speed is the kind of drug that can be so hard to get that certain people would easily kill for so much of it.

I didn't start using speed myself right away. In fact I never touched any of the drugs my father stashed at my apartment on that particular day. But eventually I decided it was time to try the stuff out. At first, I just swallowed some inside a small piece of tissue. Then I was ready to party all night.

Eventually things started falling apart at the plant where I worked, and finally, I lost my job at the plant. My new girlfriend and I decided to make a clean cut and move back to Toronto and make a go of things there. We found an apartment right in Scarborough, not far from my father's place.

At first I continued to dabble in speed without injecting or shooting because I was afraid to stick a needle in my arm. I think there was a part of me that was trying to deny the fact that I was heading down this road. Then one day I was partying with my father and some friends and I decided it was time to go for it. Everybody was getting high on speed and the pull to try it became overwhelming for me.

I only recall a few things about my first experience with a needle. I remember my heart was pounding so hard I thought I was going to have a heart attack and then the rush hit me. On my first hit of methamphetamine, I felt like Superman. The rush was intense, yet I was in total control (or so I thought). It was like a whole new world had just opened up to me. My father said "Son, now you're playing hardball." I will never forget those words as long as I live because it was true. I was playing hardball and I knew it.

My father took me around and introduced me to many of the people to whom he supplied speed, and he began showing me the world of hardcore addicts. He taught me how to read them, and showed me how to develop trusting relationships with people who I knew could never really be trusted. I began selling speed to friends and friends of friends by the gram, but soon word got out that I was connected to a pretty big source for meth, and the quantities began getting larger.

Paranoia

The closer I got to the speed subculture, the more sensitive I grew to a strange feeling of absolute darkness. At the time I could not define what it was, other than to say that I was growing more and more paranoid, so most of the time I just tried to shrug it off. In spite of my false bravado I was deeply cautious of everyone, because I sensed a dark and hidden agenda in everyone I met. Later, at the height of my paranoia, I would attribute all kinds of evil purposes to their "hidden agenda" but in reality, the main evil was that everyone just wanted to get high.

At the time I was driving a Kawasaki motorcycle, and even though I had no respect for bikers I was associated to people who were linked to them. On one occasion I made a series of trips to Kingston a couple hours east of Toronto, to help a friend make some biker connections there. Everything was great until our last trip. We had been up for so long that we needed to make a stop on the way back to shoot up. As we were about to pull off the highway I noticed a red van that looked suspicious. The people in the van looked like cops and they caught my eye as we passed them so I pulled over to the side of the road and refused to shoot any more speed. My paranoid nightmare had begun.

As part of our deal, we had to drop a gun off in a downtown Toronto hotel. As we stopped at a light I saw the red van drive by. I knew that it was the same red van I saw an hour ago on the highway. My mind was racing. Could this really be the same red van? If so, were we going to get busted? Did they know what we were up to? Were they the good guys or the bad guys? Maybe they were my father's friends watching out for me. I was tired and extremely confused. All I wanted to do was get rid of the gun and get as far away from this scene as I possibly could.

We made our connection, dropped off the gun and I drove my friend home. I was still thinking about the red van, and was freaked out all the way back to my apartment. I got up to my seventh floor apartment and went out on the balcony to reflect on the strange day it had been. To my absolute horror I watched a red van drive slowly around the parking lot below! It backed into a parking space directly below my window. A man got out of the van on the passenger side holding a paper bag in one hand, looked up to me and pointed his finger directly at me and said something I could not make out. He proceeded calmly to the lobby below. I was in absolute terror! I could only imagine that he had a gun in that paper bag, so I frantically called my dad. To my utter amazement my father told me to chill out and go to bed. I hung up the phone and sat waiting on the couch all night long with my heart pounding in stark terror. I had a hockey stick in one hand, and a knife in the other. Eventually, I fell asleep that way.

The incident with the red van came and went that night and nothing ever came of it, but it never left my mind. I continued to get deeper and deeper into the meth business and began living a life of perpetual drug addiction and fear. I used speed to get up in the morning, and downers and alcohol to come down when I was ready. All the time I was conscious of the fact that we were probably being watched by the police and I was always being watched by those who knew that I had a stash.

I continued to live a life of paranoia and addiction, and anyone who has ever been associated with meth knows that paranoia is always part of the game. The most successful speeders (if you could say such a thing) are those who learned to handle their addiction to speed and the feelings of paranoia that accompanied the drug. My father was greatly admired by other speeders because he never showed fear and was able to supply a steady stream of drugs without ever getting busted. He was "the man." I always loved my father, in spite of our family troubles, but I didn't look up to him the way others did. Yet I was amazed at the way my father could do such large quantities of methamphetamine and function almost normally, without showing fear. In this respect I was never like *my* father at all. Right from the beginning, I was paranoid and always suspicious. I was never a "good speeder."

My paranoia got worse. I recall a time when I threatened to kill my best friend because I thought he was sneaking around with my girlfriend. Later I learned from another close buddy that the person I had threatened was so afraid of me that he slept with a knife under his pillow for a month. I was becoming so pathetic and delusional that I was feared by many of the people closest to me because I was completely unpredictable.

One sunny summer afternoon, as I sat on the balcony of my apartment smoking a cigarette, I noticed a series of vans delivering some sort of equipment into the apartment building at the end of my street, a government-subsidized housing project. At the time I wasn't really concerned, as I figured that there were probably renovations or something going on in the building. I sold drugs to many people who lived there, and I knew that the whole building was filthy dirty, with the smell of urine in every stairwell, and was definitely no safe place to be at night. Eventually I began to check out these deliveries a little more carefully, and noticed that there was some writing on the side of the vans that indicated that they were delivering some kind of communications equipment. I continued to watch with curiosity and my suspicions began to grow. What could possibly be going on in that dump? Why communications equipment? Why so much of it? I thought I would keep my eye on things.

Over the next couple of weeks I began to notice what looked like CB radio antennas cropping up on the apartment balconies in the surrounding buildings. Then one day I noticed what looked like a couple of huge satellite dishes on the roof. Now I knew what the "deliveries" were all about. It didn't seem like a stretch to think that maybe the area was under police surveillance, since it was infested with crime and drugs anyway. It wasn't until I came home one sunny day and noticed two antennas attached to a balcony directly above my balcony two floors up that I realized that I was probably being watched. The antennas were far too close for comfort, and the thought of going to jail pushed my paranoia to a whole new level.

By this time, I was obviously addicted. I was concerned that going to jail would seriously cut me off from my supply of dope. I remember thinking that quitting speed was not an option, and the only way to maintain my lifestyle was to out smart the cops. My suspicions about people, places, and things took on a whole new dimension. I began to look at my own apartment to see if it might be wired for sound. After all, if I was under surveillance it only makes sense that my phone would be tapped and my apartment bugged. I went to a well-connected friend who helped me acquire some technology to detect bugs. The device was actually pretty simple. It fit in the palm of my hand and was powered by a transistor battery. It had a small antenna and a meter that would indicate the presence of any source that was transmitting radio waves within about a fifty-foot radius. I checked out my apartment and my car and found that everything around me was radioactive! To say that I was wired for sound was an understatement.

With my paranoia in high gear, I felt as though I was continually under scrutiny. It got to the point where everywhere I went I could feel the eyes upon me. When I went on the road to collect money or make a drop or something I took a pad of paper and a pen. Wherever I went, I would write license plate numbers on the pad while I drove. By the end of every trip I made, whether it was down the road to the store or across the city I would have a scribbled collection of numbers from the trip. I had pages and pages of license numbers. As strange as that sounds, some of those plate numbers actually matched up. It all seemed like a very serious game to me. It was me against them, even though I knew I could never win. But I was now addicted to the game.

I began to sense that I was not just being watched, but manipulated by forces far greater than anything I could imagine. Not only that, but I felt something much more sinister at work within these paranoid experiences. I had a desperate need to reveal the motivation behind all this scrutiny. I was never once arrested, yet I was under constant surveillance.

Late one evening, as I scanned an adjacent apartment building with high-powered binoculars, I observed someone in an apartment sitting in a chair, looking through what looked like a large telescope at another building in the area. Somehow he became aware that I was watching him and immediately closed a sophisticated blind system that made it impossible to view him further. The next night I set up a blind system of my own. I taped a piece of cardboard to the bottom half of a window in my bedroom. The cardboard had small holes cut just big enough for my binoculars to fit through. At night, with the lights out and the curtains drawn, I could sit in the darkness and watch the watchers without being detected. I actually watched as they changed shifts taking turns sitting behind that scope for hours. This was exciting!

My stories sounded insane to everyone who knew me. I was going crazy. Though I was on to something and knew it, I was also getting more and more delusional through my continual drug use. I began to isolate myself. I became even more obsessed with the need to gather evidence to prove that I was being watched. I couldn't trust anyone, so I tapped my own phone so I could listen to people from another room when they used my telephone to make a call.

I became convinced that people were entering my apartment when I would go out. So I bugged my own apartment. I had devices embedded right into the walls and floors. I rigged a stereo cabinet to automatically start recording a cassette tape when the doors of the cabinet were shut. On one occasion, I actually taped people entering my apartment within a minute after I had closed the door and left. When I played the tape back it showed that the people who were in my apartment suspected that the place was bugged and I could only hear them speak occasionally in very low whispers.

One by one, people abandoned me to my paranoid delusions. Then even my father cut me off from the drugs because I was a real liability and people were talking about how to shut me up. My girlfriend was the last person to leave me. I was getting physically abusive. During one of my explosive outbursts, I almost strangled her. On the day she left I was drinking heavily, and I passed out on the couch feeling confused and deeply depressed. I awoke to the sound of people banging on the door. I answered the door, to find a young couple to whom I had sold drugs to in the past. They were looking for some speed. I didn't have anything. One look at the state of my apartment and my mental condition, and it was obvious that I was really messed up. But those people took me in and gave me a place to stay. They told me they were going help me get cleaned up so I could get back in the game. But I knew what they really wanted. They were only interested in one thing. They knew who my father was and they were determined to get close to him. I went along anyway because I needed help. It didn't really matter to me who was offering me help or what their motivation was.

The Darkness Deepens

While I was living with these strangers I began to see another layer of my profound paranoia emerging. I began to define my paranoid experiences as dark spiritual events, even though I didn't believe in any "God" or devil. I developed the notion that the television and the radio were communicating mysterious messages related to my suspicions. The couple themselves began to fight bitterly more and more, until there was an uneasy feeling in the air whenever we were all in the same room together. Though I was suspicious of both of these folks, I was most wary of the husband. There was something very wrong with this individual. Whenever I was in his presence, I felt a tremendous sense of evil. But I suppressed these thoughts because I was paranoid and could

163

not trust my own feelings. However, I could not deny them either.

The couple had two sons. One was seven, and the other was nine. The younger boy seemed closer to his father and they seemed a lot alike. It appeared obvious to me that his father favored the young son over the older boy. I always had a special love for children, but this little boy gave me the creeps. He was extremely intelligent but had a very dark demeanour for a seven-year-old. He would play violent games with his toys for hours in front of the television set, and always seemed tuned out to the world.

One day the wife told me that she and her husband had split up and the husband had left. She asked me to watch the little boy while she slipped out for a while to score some dope, and I agreed. It was the least I could do. Anyway, I was not high on anything at the time.

The little boy was on the carpet playing in front of the television as I sat reading on a couch in the living room. He was playing quite loudly and the television was turned up. With one ear I listened to the little boy as he played, while I read a magazine. Something on the television caught my ear, and I tuned in for a moment to the cartoon the boy was watching. To my utter amazement and shock, the boy was talking to the cartoon on the television, and the cartoon seemed to be talking back!

I thought to myself, oh man, now I'm really going nuts! In complete shock I tried to regain my composure, while the little boy continued to engage in a diabolical communication with the TV! I left the room. From the end of the hall I heard the TV being turned up and the vacuum cleaner being turned on. I went back into the living room and the little boy was sitting on the floor with his finger in the end of the hose of the vacuum cleaner as he stared up at me. Now I was totally creeped out! I asked him what the heck he was doing and he replied that he was talking to his dad and getting "power."

This was off the map! I didn't know what to think. I moved closer to him to try to get him to shut the vacuum cleaner off, but in a loud voice the little boy began saying "he's too powerful, I can't do it." I strained to understand what was going on, then, I heard it myself! I heard the voice of his father, yelling to his son that he had the power to beat me and he could destroy me if he wanted! The little boy's father was not in the room or in the building at all, yet I could hear him distinctly as if he was nearby. This was way too weird for me! I was overcome with a powerful sense of supernatural evil in the room. My mind began to race and my heart started pounding. What was going on here? Was this all in my head? How could this be happening? I just heard it with my own ears and saw it with my eyes! What "power" was he talking about? Was it even real? Not only was I paranoid, but I was going completely crazy too. But this was now my reality and I had no choice but to try to survive it. It wasn't long until the little boy's mother came home and I left the apartment to think about the darkness that was consuming me.

Day by day, paranormal experiences persisted, regardless of whether I was drunk, stoned or straight. Though they seemed far more powerful when I was high, they persisted and grew darker. What had begun, as an exhilarating venture into what I thought would be an alternative lifestyle as a drug dealer, became a gradual descent into a treacherous living nightmare. My mind, my soul, and my very existence became completely absorbed by the nightmare I was living.

I became extremely sensitive to the supernatural forces all around me to the point where I communicated openly with the darkness. I developed a form of communication with the dark forces through taps in the wall. I would ask yes or no questions to the dark forces and there would be an audible replay in the form of tapping or a rapping in the wall. Two taps meant "yes" and one tap meant "no." I came to know that the shadows concealed a hidden reality. Little by little I discovered that my comfortable interpretation of human reality, based on my experiences of life, had actually distracted me from a deeper reality – supernatural reality. I had an ominous feeling that the dark forces I was becoming more and more aware of, had a very sinister purpose that was rooted in pure evil. But what was the reason for it all? What did these dark forces want? Who were they? Was there a devil? If so, why? Why became the question that would drive me mad and eventually save my soul.

Though I was becoming more and more sensitive to paranormal events around me I had never really asked the hard questions of meaning and purpose. Since my first experiences I was far too preoccupied with the actual reality of the supernatural events that were taking place to think about the reasons. I had all that I could deal with just trying to maintain my sanity in the midst of the reality of a scary supernatural side to life that was manifesting daily. However, I eventually began to develop a powerful curiosity about the nature of my experiences. In saner moments I would go to bookstores or libraries to try to learn something about them.

I had no preconceived notions of religion or spirituality, so I sought answers to my experiences through books written about the paranormal. For the most part, books that dealt with the paranormal always seemed shallow and silly and fake. Aside from dark shadows that seemed to move in the night and the boogieman under the bed when I was a child, I never believed in anything I could not see with my own two eyes. All my life I had no basis for a belief in the supernatural and therefore I had no context for these dark experiences. However, I stumbled across an article in an encyclopedia on the occult that finally confirmed my experiences as something that was rooted in an undeniable reality. I read a small piece on the Fox Sisters in Hydesville, New York in the mid 1800's who were said to communicate with spirits through rappings in the wall. Though the sisters were considered to be frauds I knew that these rappings were very real because I consulted them on a daily basis. I considered this story as an absolute confirmation of my own experiences.

The way that I viewed my reality began to shift. Without a religious or spiritual background in my life I had little or no basic knowledge of the Bible or any other defined belief system for that matter. Now I was a believer, but what did I believe? I didn't know.

It wasn't until a few years after I regained my sanity that my brother told me of an experience involving one my episodes that shook him to the core. From time to time I would stay at my mother's small bachelor apartment in Toronto, as she was one of the only people who could handle my insanity. One evening my younger brother slept on the couch at her apartment while I slept on the floor. Late at night I would hear "mysterious people" or "spirits" speak to me from the apartment next to my mother's. On this particular night I could hear people coming up the elevator and go to the apartment next door. Having experienced numerous diabolical communications with "strange people" or "spirits" in the past I said out loud to my mother and brother that the "evil spirits where here". I lay in the darkness while the "evil spirits" in the next apartment taunted me and tapped on the walls. As usual, I thought I was insane and maybe the "spirits" next door didn't even exist and was just an evil figment of my imagination. I was to find out years later that my brother had actually heard the "spirits" or "mysterious people" that night. He confided to me years later that it was the single scariest moment of his life.

I became addicted to the episodes of evil. I continued to use meth whenever I could because the darkness seemed much more vivid when I was high on speed. The addiction to drugs became a secondary issue in comparison to my addiction to finding clues to the darkness. Day and night I obsessed over the question of, why? Why was this all happening to me? Did I offend some divine power so deeply that I deserved to live in a continual nightmare? Did I somehow stumble on supernatural secrets so powerful that I deserved an eternal curse of eternal darkness? By now all concern for the police, or jail or any other natural consequences for my behaviour was insignificant compared to the supernatural curse that I was under. Everything was evil to me. Every experience, every moment became filled with despair, confusion, and darkness. But then, right when I thought there was no answer to my cursed existence, I had a profoundly evil experience. I wasn't alone. This time, someone else experienced the evil with me.

It was late one night at my mother's apartment. I was listening to voices that seemed to come from an apartment directly below my mother's. It sounded like a number of people were in the room, and I heard an eerie sound like something walking in the apartment below. The noise it made sounded like that of hoofs on the floor below. I thought that maybe it was high-heeled shoes, but the quality of the sound reminded me of hoofs. I listened as the group of "people" got into the elevator below and was coming toward my mother's floor. They got off the elevator and entered the apartment next door and began to play rock and roll music. As I heard *Credence Clearwater Revival* playing in the background, I strained to listen as I had done many times before, but this time something was different. I lay in the darkness, listening to the music playing from behind the wall. There seemed to be more "strange people" or "spirits" than before, almost as if they were having a party next door.

As the music played, I heard familiar voices start to taunt me and laugh at my frustration. I was so fed up with the curse and so confused by this evil that my fears became sec-

168

ondary. As I listened, an evil voice spoke clearly to me, the voice of a diabolical old lady; and she told me that she had been "waiting a long time for me" to come. She said that her husband was gone and she was here to marry me! My heart was beating so loud that I almost heard it in my chest. Not knowing what else to say, I spoke up and said "if you want to marry me, what shall I do?" The voice replied "get dressed and step outside the door."

In utter fear and profound confusion, I jumped up and reached for the first thing I found – a Bible! At this point my mother jumped out of bed and turned all the lights on, and we listened to the voices in the next apartment jeering and laughing. My mother listened in extreme terror. All at once, I could see that she realized everything I had been saying all along was true! She ran to her dresser and grabbed a big black family Bible and screamed at the top of her lungs that they could not have her son! I was reading out loud from the Bible for the first time in my life! To this day I do not know what I was reading, but every word that I read from that Bible seemed to speak profoundly to the situation. I came across a passage that caused me to say, "In the name of Jesus Christ, I rebuke you and I command you to leave this place!" At that time I did not know what I was saying, and I did not even know what the word "rebuke" even meant! All at once everything was quiet and the apartment was filled with silence. I heard a voice break the silence and say, "Oh no, we're going to die." Not a word was spoken as the people got into the elevator and left the building. In the dead of night, I could hear them walking on the street below. I sat frozen in a mixture of fear and confused disbelief. My mother was crying and deeply shaken. We have rarely spoken of this night since it happened, and I believe she has all but erased it from her memories – a thing I can never do.

In the days and weeks that followed that terrifying night, I was continually haunted by it. For the life of me, I could not understand what it meant. I replayed the events over and over in my head and I continued to use drugs to try to conjure up similar events in the hopes that I would find some clue to my nightmare, but there were no answers. By this time, I was pretty much cut off from all methamphetamine, and I began to inject cocaine as it had similar stimulant effects. It made things worse. I became horribly addicted and it only seemed make me more confused.

In spite of the fact that my girlfriend had left me and made it clear that we would never be together again, I also obsessed over my love for her when I wasn't thinking about drugs or evil. In the few fleeting moments when I wasn't thinking of drugs, evil, or my girlfriend, I despaired over my love for my son.

Day by day, and hour by hour, my sanity was slipping through my hands as I watched it go. All the curiosity that I had once had about the nature of these paranormal events was no longer important to me. The reasons for my curse didn't matter. The only thing that mattered to me now was that I was lost, and there was no way out. My soul was being destroyed. I despaired deeply at my own curse, but what made my curse even more depressing was that I knew all of humanity was under the same curse – and no one knew. Though I didn't know all of the reasons why, I came to realize that there are forces in this world that exist in the shadows. There are supernatural forces at work to destroy the human soul. My curse is our curse, and I could not tell anyone. They could not believe it.

At the very depth of my despair, I came to the point where I could not bear the burden any longer. I began to think about the only answer to my suffering, suicide. I had been through a lot in my life, and never once, ever thought of killing myself. I was beyond all hope. I simply needed to get rid of the pain. I felt like a cancer patient who was in severe agony and death was the only option left. I tried to convince myself that death was not an option but I could not truly live.

To me, my life was over. Every waking moment was filled with fear and grief and I could not bear it any longer.

I began to think of what would happen to those who loved me, and what my death would do to them. Although it bothered me that my family would feel the shame of my suicide, I felt like most people had abandoned me already and my leaving would not hurt them much. I thought about my girlfriend, and I figured that she would be okay since she didn't want to be with me anyway. In a strange way, I thought my death would eventually bring her peace. When I thought about my son, it broke my heart. I would leave him a legacy of shame and destruction, and he would have to bear the burden of it his whole life.

But I made up my mind that death was the only way to put a stop to the pain and confusion I was feeling. So I began to think of ways to die. Jumping off my mother's apartment balcony was not an option, because I could not stand the thought of falling to my death, and I did not want to leave a mess. I thought of overdosing myself with my mother's pills, but I did not want to leave her with the guilt of providing the means to my suicide. I decided that I would go to the subway station and jump in front of a train. Even though it would be messy, I thought it would be quick and relatively painless. There would be no long goodbye letters or final phone calls. This was something I had to do for myself, and I had to be courageous enough to face my own death. It was all over for me.

A Hope in Hell

The day that I was to die was filled with sadness. I was at my mother's apartment, and I tried to sit with her for a while, hoping to find ways to tell her somehow that I loved her, and to make her understand that my death would not be her fault. In the state I was in I could not do any of those things without letting her know what I was planning to do, so I said nothing. As the hour grew near when I would make my way to the subway station, I became overwhelmed with grief. Mentally, spiritually and emotionally I was preparing to die, and the sadness of leaving this world behind was too much to bear. I began to go over all of the bad things I had done in my life, no matter how big or how small. I tried to recall every event in which I had hurt someone or something, no matter how insignificant it might seem. I began to weep as I realized how sinful I really was. In my preparation for my death I called out to God for the first time ever. All my life I had never believed there was a God, but now it was obvious to me that God did exist. My grandmother had told me about God as I was growing up and her stories were the only information I had to go on. On this day, of all days, I needed God's forgiveness. It was my last-ditch effort to be honest with myself, and somehow to repent before I died.

The more I thought about myself and my evil ways, the more I cried out to God. I sat in the middle of my mother's kitchen weeping like a child. I never spoke a word out loud, but in my heart I cried out to God with all of my soul to forgive me for my wretched ways. My mourning over my death turned into a grueling assessment of my sinful life. The more I uncovered my sins, the more I realized my wretchedness, and the more I saw my unworthiness to even approach God with my sins; but I was damned and there was nothing else I could do! As I cried out to God I pleaded with Him to reveal Himself to me because it was the day I would die. I begged God to show me He was real in a way that I could understand, and I asked Him to heal me if He would. I told Him that I could make no promises to Him except the promise to try the best I could, even though I knew that even this promise was a weak one. As I realized the weight of my request I realized I was asking Him to heal me – and to do it all on His own, because I knew that I was that weak. As I cried out to God, a puddle of tears was forming on the floor, and I was sweating all over. Finally, after what seemed like two hours or more, I was exhausted. I could not cry anymore. My face was sore. My stomach muscles were sore and I had no more tears. I got up from the floor and lay on my mother's couch. I looked at her where she sat watching TV, as she did through this whole episode.

It was a summer afternoon in August of 1986. It was very cloudy outside and there was a light drizzle and fog in the air as my mother's apartment building was in the beaches area of Toronto. Exhausted, I was staring blankly at the clouds out her balcony window. As I lay on the couch I felt a physical sensation like that of waves washing over me. As I stared up into the sky a strange vision started to form in the clouds. As I watched in amazement, something that looked like three white stairs began to appear before me. I looked away and shook my head, but the vision in the clouds remained. Then, as I gazed into the clouds, they seemed to be parting just above the top stair and the sun sent a glimmering ray of light down toward earth! I could only think that this was some sort of illusion or hallucination that I was having. Then it struck me: I had asked God to reveal Himself to me in a way that I could understand. I actually began to think that maybe God was going to walk out of those clouds and come down the three stairs! I was terrified, and my knees began to knock.

As I stared at the clouds a seagull flew out of the middle, just where they had parted above the stairs. I watched as the seagull flew around and then went off into the distance. I looked back at the stairs and they slowly vaporized and melted into the clouds. The clouds closed up and it started to rain again. Suddenly, I felt different. I knew that the vision I just had in the clouds was from God, but I didn't know what it meant. As I sat on my mother's couch thinking about what had just taken place, I realized that I was completely well again! I will never be able to explain the moment except to say I had an extreme feeling of well-being and profound potential! All of my evil delusions and thoughts of suicide were gone, and I didn't know why! I knew that God had just visited me, but I had no idea what it all meant and I was struggling to believe it was all real. It was real! I could feel it! But what did it mean? I recall feeling utterly overwhelmed and happy, but I also knew that I was crazy, so only a small part of me cautiously believed that all of this was for real. All that afternoon and into the evening I felt a strange, powerful sense of healing and wellness, and I thought to myself the real test would be if I woke up the next day feeling the same way. That night I slept like a baby, and the next day I woke up with the same sense of wellness and extreme potential. Though I had been haunted by questions of evil and the diabolical nightmare I was living, now I felt an extreme sense of divinity and hope.

My mother knew nothing of this. One afternoon she asked me to go to the store across the street and get her a quart of milk for her tea. I went across the street to the variety store, as I had done countless times before. As I approached the store a little old lady was walking down the street handing out Bible tracts to passers by. I took a tract without a word, and put it in my back pocket. I bought my mother her milk and went back home. I sat thinking about the weird and wonderful experiences of the last couple days. Then I began to read a Bible that my grandmother had left lying around my mother's apartment. My grandmother had been an ex-alcoholic who had come to a deep abiding faith in Jesus Christ. At every opportunity she would tell anyone who would listen about her conversion from alcohol to faith. She loved my mother greatly, and had a deep desire to see her find Christ. Whenever she visited my mother she would leave Christian magazines or Bibles behind. As I sat reading one of those Bibles and thinking about what it all meant it dawned on me! Maybe the Bible tract that I was given would provide some clue to the vision in the clouds. I searched for that tract until I found it and I was absolutely shocked by the drawing on the front cover. There was a picture of clouds parting while the sun broke through the clouds with a seagull flying through the opening! The exact picture of my vision in the clouds! There was writing in bold letters on the cover of the tract "The Steps to Salvation."

As I opened the tract in astonishment I read the three steps to salvation – "repent, believe, and follow." In utter amazement I realized all at once and beyond any shadow of doubt that I was in the presence of God almighty! My head swam with pure delight as I felt the very presence of God in that small apartment. In sheer beauty and power, full of grace and absolute truth, God almighty was speaking to me! I laughed out loud as I began to realize that God had answered all my prayers in a way that was far too amazing to be any kind of delusion or cosmic coincidence. The more I thought about it, the more profound my experience was becoming. Earlier I had asked God to reveal Himself in a way that I could understand. I prayed to Him to reveal Himself in a way that would be clear to me. I asked Him to show Himself and His plan in a way that would make sense to me and leave no doubt in my mind. God was answering all my prayers! As I read that simple little piece of paper, I knew that I had discovered God, and somehow I knew that everything in my life was going to be all right! I knew from that moment on that God would continue to speak to me and He would show me the way to live out my life. Though I knew little about the Bible, I knew at that moment that the Bible would bring me life and reveal God to me until the very day that I died.

I wish that I could say that I lived a victorious, clean, drug free life ever since the day that God first revealed Himself to me, but that would be a lie. The fact is, following that day of revelation I struggled with the needle and my commitment to the truth for almost three years. I had been living my life in sin for so long, and my profound weakness for getting high made it almost impossible for me to turn my life around right away. So for a couple of years I kicked around at odd jobs and struggled with sin and battled the demons in my life. I knew that I had faith, I sensed an awesome potential for my life, and God was a daily reality to me, but I knew that I lacked a total commitment. Even though I tried to curb my appetite for sin, I continued to struggle and I still did drugs. I had fleeting moments of victory, but I lived with a nagging uncomfortable feeling in my soul that haunted me day and night. Every time I got high, I knew there was another way to live my life. I knew that God had done something great that day in the clouds, and I knew that somehow, I was denying God and wasting His tremendous gift to me.

Eventually, I got too sick of living a diminished, half-hearted life. God was constantly calling me deeper into a spiritual life and His presence was strong with me. Finally, I got to the point where I could not continue to live in sin anymore and I got on my knees and gave my whole life over to God. I began by putting away the major sins in my life and living for God one hour at a time. As hours turned to days and days turned to weeks, I systematically began to work on all of the bad behaviours that I knew kept me from God. I prayed long hours and read the Bible. I began to hunger for God's Word and His presence in a way that consumed my life.

All of the people closest to me thought I was just going through a phase. Little did they know that God was actually changing me. I recall a time when I was struggling with my new life, and living with my pregnant wife, and we had no rent money and the food was running out. God just told me to pray. My wife was getting upset because all we had was a bag of potatoes and quart of milk, and rent was due in two weeks. I told my wife that God would make a way, but we needed to trust Him. At first she was furious, but I convinced her to trust my faith if she didn't have her own faith. I told her that God told me to do nothing but pray, and that if I was wrong then her anger would be completely justified. Reluctantly, she agreed and decided to wait to see if anything would happen.

God told me to stay home the next day and just pray and trust Him entirely for everything, so the next day I stayed home and prayed instead of looking for work. The next day at around ten o'clock in the morning I received a phone call from a lady a couple of blocks away. She told me that she was having family come over from Europe in two weeks and she needed the interior of her house painted right away! I couldn't believe my ears! I asked her how she got my phone number and she told me that she received a flyer in the mail a year earlier advertising a house painter and she threw the flyer in the kitchen drawer! Again, a powerful answer to prayer. It was this experience that showed me that God could be trusted in every situation and that He would make the way for my life to change. All I had to do was exercise faith.

As I exercised my faith daily, my spiritual strength grew. Things that once seemed impossible for me were now just a matter of faith. I came to know that anything was possible for me if it was God's will for my life. My life was no longer defined by the things I wanted, but all of life was defined by God's will and His purposes. As I dealt with my sin, little by little I was learning that God was changing me for His purposes. I began to view life in terms of God's Kingdom, and my whole understanding of the purpose for life became centered on the potential for faith. Faith was the key for me, and I soon realized that the whole purpose for human life was rooted in each person's relationship to God.

The Road Up

I recall a powerful teaching that God revealed to me that profoundly changed the way I understood my own life and redefined my thoughts about the drug addiction that had always plagued my life. A couple of years after I had focused my life on Christ, I had a major slip. I had been drug free for a couple of years, and was growing in leaps and bounds in faith. But then I found myself drawn back to the needle. After sticking a needle in my arm for the first time in two years, I sat in the darkness with profound feelings of shame and guilt and deep depression over what I had just done. God spoke. In the darkness in my basement, God's Spirit spoke to me in a quiet but powerful manner. He provoked me to think deeply about who I was. As I began to feel the old feelings of being a hopeless drug addict and a total loser, God told me I was His child. I had heard many sermons and teachings about believers being God's children through faith, but this was different. God showed me that I could never be defined in any other way. In other words, I was not just some person, I was actually God's child. I was not a drug addict, and could never be a drug addict, because I was God's child and I had to fulfill His purposes. As these thoughts of sonship started to sink in to my heart and mind I prayed for forgiveness for my mistake. God made His forgiveness powerfully clear that day, and in small, miraculous ways, He confirmed His teaching to me that I was His child and not a drug addict. That was one of the most powerful insights I had ever learned. I was a child of God. I was destined to live my life as His child. Nothing could ever change that fact. It was this single insight that opened my eyes to a new future and gave me strength for this journey.

God's presence in my life was obvious to everyone around me, and everyone who knew me saw the profound changes in me. A couple years after I had come to faith I felt a deep call to do volunteer work with inmates in order to share the profound truth I had discovered. I wrote a letter to the government, and applied to have my criminal record cleared. Six months later a pardon came in the mail. The possibilities were endless!

Other changes were coming too. Once, the idea of going back to school was far too unappealing to even consider, but now the idea was growing in my mind. Once, my low self-esteem, my inadequate education and my history with drugs and crime would have prevented me from ever thinking that I could achieve a university degree. Now I knew that anything was possible through faith, and I was being called to live up to God's leading. God began to work the idea of prison Chaplaincy into my mind, but the thought of going back to school still scared me to the core. After all, I had not even made it half way through grade nine. However, with God's help and His leading, I was confronting all of the fears and failures in my life and school was a mountain that God was calling me to climb.

As I applied myself to overcoming all of my fears through faith, God was carving out a new life for me. I was being confronted day and night by thoughts of working with inmates, because I knew that there were so many desperate souls languishing in jail. So I began to apply myself through faith and the doors started opening up wide. I struggled with college for three years, and received a bachelor's degree in religious education. Though school was a tremendous challenge, I actually thrived on the rigors of theological enlightenment. Still, school was probably the single greatest test of my faith because it challenged all of my assumptions. I consumed my studies with great enthusiasm.

God was calling me to be a Chaplain, and the challenge before me was extremely exciting. After my undergraduate studies at Ontario Bible College (now known as Tyndale University College), I needed to continue with a graduate degree in order to become a chaplain. It took me three more years to get a Master's Degree in Theological Studies, which I did with the same vigor and enthusiasm. The challenge to learn and grow in my Christian understanding was so exciting that I made the most of the opportunity that God had given me. I wanted to learn, and not just get my grades, so I purposely chose a university that was known internationally for its academic standards. In 1997 I received a Master's Degree in Theological Studies from the University of St Michael's College at the Toronto School of Theology at the University of Toronto. I didn't graduate with honors, but I did graduate with a profound sense of accomplishment and the knowledge that God was with me every step of the way. All the honour and the glory must go to God alone, because it was He who brought me from dirty needles in a back alley to the sacred study of divine truth and the pursuit of His holiness.

I believe that the dark experiences of my past have made it hard for me to fully express the love God has shown to me, but my relationship with God has even made it possible for me to have loving relationships. God has blessed me with so much in this life that this story would not be complete without mentioning what it means for someone like me to know real family love.

Before I had known God's presence in my life, it would have been impossible to maintain the relationships that are now such a big part of my life. When I was lost in drug addiction and spiritual darkness, having an authentic relationship was out of the question. Many times I had tried to imagine what it would be like to have a good family and to be content, but all of this seemed way out of my reach. When I thought about these things it only made me depressed because I believed that I was too far gone to ever have the real experience of family love. However, as I grew away from my old life and lived out the new life to which God was calling me, He added things that I could never have imagined. The more that I applied myself to live a clean and faithful life, the more I received from God.

I had made a huge mess of my first marriage, but I had maintained my relationship with my son and his mother.

In spite of my mistakes, I was given another chance at a new marriage and an even larger family, with more love than I ever could have thought possible. During the years that I was preparing myself to work as a chaplain, my wife and I had three children (who are all now teenagers). We brought up our children and fostered other children in our home. Due to my wife's background in social work and child-care, we eventually took in a number of troubled teens. Altogether, we cared for over one hundred children in our eleven years as foster parents. I was able to identify with these children because of my own background, while my wife was able to approach fostering from a more clinical perspective. This proved to be a good combination for helping out damaged (and often hard-nosed) teenagers.

Fostering was very rewarding at times, but if I'm honest, the victories were very few and far between. We learned that the children we fostered craved love, but they also needed structure. While we weren't too strict, we provided our foster children with fair, healthy boundaries while we tried to love them as best we could. This meant that our house was always a battleground, because we felt that our job was to prepare all of our kids for the real world. One thing you learn about foster children is that many are so hurt that most never really understand what you are trying to do for them – just as I could not see what my own foster family had once tried to do for me. However, the good news is that there were some children who connected with us deeply, and those children became like our own.

Today, at every Christmas, Thanksgiving and Easter, we enjoy great celebrations of love and life. At our house there is always a big table, with lots of food, where everyone is welcome. Now I can honestly say I experience God's presence in every moment, and I have a huge abundance of family love. I have found a deep sense of purpose and contentment in my life. I am not saying that I don't suffer at all, because

I still struggle in many ways, but God has poured out His blessings on me and surpassed anything I could imagine.

It is the love and contentment of knowing God in my life, and of having a wonderful wife and a good family that help me to stay away from the things that are so harmful. When I remember the great darkness that controlled my life and nearly destroyed me, I thank God for every good blessing that has come to me in these later years. There was a time when life was like a nightmare, all of my dreams were dark, and all of my hopes turned out bad. Now God has given me a new heart and a new life, one in which anything is possible. Life is not perfect, and I still struggle with sin. In fact, the struggle with sin will always be the hardest part of living, but it is possible to deal with it. But the thing we need to see is that our sin must be dealt with first, if we are ever to find this kind of love and contentment.

The Road Ahead

Most of the people I talk to who are in bondage to drugs and crime think it's impossible to accomplish anything good, or find love and contentment because of their past failures. It is to those people that I offer my story. My life has been scarred by the failures of my past, and I know that I will always carry some of those scars with me. But it is the great struggle with sin and failure that has brought me life and blessed my soul forever, because God has met me with His love. It was my failure and my sin that ultimately caused me to turn to God in desperation, and when I finally turned to Him I found love. Once, my life was marked by sin, failure, and rebellion, which only produced death and destruction for me. However, God's great and glorious love confronted all of the death and destruction in my life, and now my life is marked by faith, love and hope. It is faith, love and hope that

John Anderson at Annual Dinner 2005

give life meaning and purpose, especially for those who have destroyed their own lives through sin.

Ultimately, it is our sin and failure that causes us to turn to something greater than ourselves, and when we turn from ourselves we find Jesus Christ. Through Jesus' sacrifice on the cross, there is freedom from sin because He destroyed sin's power. Sin's power is death. It is sin that holds all of us in bondage because sin destroys our lives and separates us from God's love. Because of our appetite for sin we never even know that there is a God who loves us and wants us to have a beautiful life and an extraordinary experience of faith. Drug addicts, criminals and failures (according to this world's standards) seem furthest from God because they are people who have given themselves over to their own sinful weaknesses and temptations. In reality, the farther we are from God, the greater the chance that we are at the end of ourselves. It is at the end of ourselves that we find God. My hope and prayer is for those who are at the end of themselves. I offer you this story in the hope that you begin to take a hard look at yourself and then at God. I pray that this story will call you to look to God in spite of the mess that you have made of your life. I pray that this story will encourage you to think about God and look to Him as a source of real hope and possibility.

Finally, I leave you with one word. In all of my struggles with sin and failure and in everything I've ever learned from the pursuit of higher knowledge and perfect Biblical truth, there is one word that brings meaning and purpose to life. I leave you with the word "surrender." It is only surrender that matters in this life. There is no way to overcome sin without surrender. There is no hope for life or love, or a relationship with God without surrender. Surrender to God whatever it takes. Surrender now and surrender completely. Surrender your life and surrender your hope. It's that simple. Surrender is the way to God and the road to true freedom from sin.

John Anderson

Peace with God

1. To have peace with God is an extraordinary event in a person's life. The first step is to become acquainted with God's plan of salvation which brings a person complete peace.

God loves you and wants you to have peace and eternal life.

The Bible says:

"...We have peace with God through our Lord Jesus Christ." **(Romans 5:1)**

"For God so loved the world, that he gave His only begotten Son, that whosoever believeth in Him should not perish but have everlasting life." **(John 3:16)**

"...I am come that they might have life, and that they might have it more abundantly." **(John 10:10)**

God wants man to have peace and an abundant life, but many people live their lives in such a way that does not bring them peace.

2. Man must realize his *problem of separation from God.* God created man in His own image and likeness and gave him a wonderful life. God did not make man a robot which would automatically love God, involuntarily fulfilling His will. God gave man a free choice between good and evil.

Mankind chose for itself the path of disobedience to God and lives without God. Man always had and even now has the power of choosing between good and evil. Choosing the evil way leads to *separation* from God.

MAN (sinful)	GOD (Holy)

The Bible says:

"For all have sinned and come short of the glory of God." **(Romans 3:23)**

"For the wages of sin is death; but the gift of God is eternal life through Jesus Christ our Lord." **(Romans 6:23)**

Throughout the ages mankind has unsuccessfully endeavoured to bridge this gulf which separates him from God.

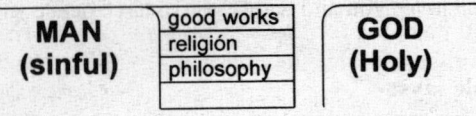

In this world there exists only one solution to this problem of separation from God.

3. Acknowledge *God's way – The Cross of Calvary* Jesus Christ is the only way out of this disastrous situation of separation from God. This separation lies as a gulf between God and man. Christ gave Himself over in order to liberate us. He died on the cross, but through His resurrection from the dead He bridged the gulf between God and man. His death and resurrection gives new life to all of those who believe in Him.

God stands on one side of this gulf and all mankind on the other. Jesus Christ, the God-man, is the bridge over this terrifying gulf and His intercession renews the broken union between God and man.

The Bible says:
"But God commendeth His love toward us, in that, while we were yet sinners, Christ died for us." **(Romans 5:8)**

"Jesus saith unto him, I am the way, the truth and the life: no man cometh unto the Father, but by me." (John 14:6)

"For by grace are ye saved through faith; and that not of yourselves: it is the gift of God: Not of works, lest any man should boast." (Ephesians 2:8-9)

God provides for us the *only way*. Every person must decide for himself what he will do with Christ.

4. You must now make your decision: accept or reject Jesus Christ. We have to trust Christ and personally accept Him into our heart.

Are you here   or   here?

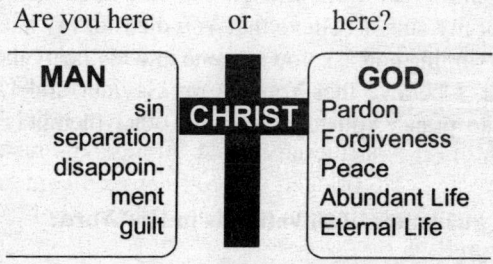

MAN	CHRIST	GOD
sin		Pardon
separation		Forgiveness
disappoin-		Peace
ment		Abundant Life
guilt		Eternal Life

The Bible says:

"Behold I stand at the door and knock: if any man hear my voice, and open the door, I will come in to him, and will sup with him, and he with Me." (Revelation 3:20)

"But as many as received Him, to them gave He power to become the sons of God; even to them that believe on His name." (John 1:12)

"That if thou shalt confess with thy mouth the Lord Jesus and shalt believe in thine heart that God hath raised Him from the dead, thou shalt be saved." (Romans 10:9)

What is stopping you from now accepting Jesus Christ as your personal Saviour?

187

What you must do:

1. Acknowledge that you are a sinner.

2. Repent.

3. Believe, that Christ died for you on the cross and rose from the dead.

4. Accept Christ as your personal Saviour.

How to pray:

Dear Lord,

I know that I am a lost sinner and need Your forgiveness for my sins. I believe that You died for my sins. I want to stop sinning and ask you to come into my heart and change my life. I believe that You are my Saviour and Lord, and desire to praise You together with other members of Your Church.

God's guarantee of salvation is in His Word:

Did you pray this prayer?

The Bible says:

"For all who call upon the name of the Lord shall be saved." **(Romans 10:13)**

Did you ask Christ to become your Lord and Saviour? In what kind of state do you now find yourself?

The Bible says:

"He that hath the Son hath life; and he that hath not the Son of God hath not life. These things have I written unto you that believe on the name of the Son of God; that ye may know that ye have eternal life, and that ye may believe on the name of the Son of God." **(1 John 5:12,13)**

How You Can Live A Successful Christian Life

God bless you! Along with the angels in heaven (Luke 14:10), I rejoice that you've trusted Jesus Christ for the forgiveness of your sins and are ready to live a new life through Him. Here are some things the Bible says are important to know about your new relationship with Him.

First, *always trust* that, no matter what, you've received eternal life through Christ (1 John 5:10-13). Then, by faith, walk in newness of life with Him (Romans 6:4, 1 Timothy 6:12). Remember, *the Christian life is not an imitation of Christ, but the new, resurrection life of Christ manifested in your life.* "He that believeth in the Son hath everlasting life" (John 3:36).

Second, *read* your Bible daily. *Memorize* passages that are meaningful to you, especially the promises. *Think a lot* about them. They will be *food* to your soul (1 Peter 2: 2), a *light* to show you the way to live your life (Psalm 119: 105), and the weapons you need to fight temptation and sin (Ephesians 6:17).

Third, *pray daily* to God in the name of Jesus Christ. *Thank Him* for everything in your life, remembering that your blessings are His gifts to you. Always keep in mind that you can sin at any time, so *pray for help and victory.* "They that wait upon the Lord shall renew their strength" (Isaiah 40:31).

Fourth, *avoid temptation.* Temptation is a part of everyone's life, but now that Christ lives within you, you have the power to overcome them (Romans 6:1-14). *Avoid* evil people and make friends with God's people. Remember,

God promises to never allow you to be tempted beyond your ability to resist, so *trust Him* to show you a way to escape the temptation (1 Corinthians 10:13). Always yield to him and trust Him for victory.

Fifth, *regularly attend* a church of your choice, but make sure it faithfully teaches God's Word (Hebrews 10: 25). You will find strength and encouragement in Christian fellowship (Romans 1:12-13).

Decision Card

Convinced I am a guilty, lost sinner, and believing that Christ died for my sins and rose again from the dead for me, I now receive Him as my personal Saviour, and with His help, I will tell everyone I can about Him.

Name _____

Date _____

If you'd like further information or wish to talk with someone about your newfound faith, feel free to contact me or any of the men you've read about in this book.

God Bless You!